Pattern Glass
MUGS

by John B. Mordock & Walter L. Adams

DEDICATION

This book is dedicated to four ladies. First and foremost to our wives, Nancy Mordock and Linda Adams. Without their patience and support of our "obsession," this book would not have been possible. Also to Marjorie Tingley, who spent countless hours using her extraordinary library to help provide references, and to Mollie Helen McCain, who provided sketches when no photographs were available.

The following are individuals who contributed to making this book possible:

Bill & Betty Annable - *Oberlin, Ohio*
Chris & Helene Bauman - *Oswego, Illinois*
William F. Bigoney - *Ft. Lauderdale, Florida*
Scott Brown - *Grand Rapids, Michigan*
Corinne Creighton - *Ft. Lauderdale, Florida*
Diane Eagan - *Colgate, Wisconsin*
Harold Essmaker - *Mt. Clemens, Michigan*
Perry Fisk - *Ft. Lauderdale, Florida*
Dr. Adam Fikso - *Glenview, Illinois*
Dr. Anna Lee Fjellberg - *Glenview, Illinois*
Helen Foster - *Ft. Lauderdale, Florida*
Brandt M. Godleski - *Pompano, Florida*
Helen Goldberg - *Pittsboro, North Carolina*
Lola Higby - *Ventura, California*
Bill Jenks - *Kingston, Pennsylvania*
Ken Kerchival - *Los Angeles, California*
Doris Langerman - *Highland Park, Illinois*
Terry Mackey - *Carlisle, Pennsylvania*
Lil & Bud Marchet - *Yarmouth, Massachusetts*
Mollie H. McCain - *Grand Rapids, Michigan*
Jesse McManus - *Hillsboro, Wisconsin*
William B. Miller - *Plantation, Florida*
Tom Neal - *Bridgewater, Virginia*
Kirk Nelson - *Sandwich, Massachusetts*
Bert Nunneley - *Mt. Clemens, Michigan*
Linda Sandell, *Minneapolis, MN*
Glen Schotfeld - *Bridgewater, Virginia*
Mark Schuster - *Madison, Wisconsin*
Carmen Slater - *Oconomowoc, Wisconsin*
Nancy Smith - *Grand Rapids, Michigan*
Maryln Strauss - *Winnetka, Illinois*
Warren Tingley - *Deerfield Beach, Florida*
Jerry Wood - *DeQuincy, Louisiana*
Mike Zimmerman - *Northbrook, Illinois*

The following institutions were helpful in providing information and pictures:

The National Heisey Glass Museum
Newark, Ohio

The Sandwich Glass Museum
Sandwich, Massachusetts

We thank the following people for allowing us to use material from their books:

Mr. & Mrs. Thomas Cronin
"Early American Pattern Glass"
books I & II, by Alice H. Metz

Stan Gores
"1876 Centennial Collectibles"
Dale K. Graham - Publisher of Antiques and Collecting Magazine

THE GLASS PRESS, INC. • dba Antique Publications • Post Office Box 553 • Marietta, Ohio 45750
PB ISBN #1-57080-010-3 HB ISBN #1-57080-011-1

54. LION HUNT

CONTENTS

PREFACE

It is hoped that this book will appeal to the reader on several levels. It is intended to be a picture book suitable for casual browsing. It is also intended to be used for identification purposes by glass collectors and dealers. To make both of these functions easier, special attention has been given to providing clear and identifiable photographs.

Another level upon which we hope to assist the reader is finding the "What," the "Where" and the "Why" of glass patterns. The most reliable information is from original glass company catalogues and advertisements. Wherever possible, we have referred to these catalogues and advertisements or employed reference works that use such sources. We also have used reference works that give pattern information based on shards dug from the glass factories. Interviews with former glass factory workers and family histories have also been utilized. In some cases, we were unable to verify the information source used by the reference works. When no references were available, assumptions and speculations have been made. However, they are just that and should not be taken for fact.

Since some mugs have many names and the original names for others are totally unknown, the mugs are arranged in this book by subject matter to make identification easier. The category in which a mug is listed will be the one in which the dominate feature or features fit best. When a name is unknown, the reference will say "None". In this case we have provided a descriptive name. In the past, some authors named patterns for people or places they wanted to honor when the original name was unknown. While this is a nice gesture, it only adds to the confusion of identification. The practice that should be observed is to give the original manufacturer's name and/or a descriptive name. Other names that have been in common usage for many years have also been included.

Diameters and heights of these mugs may vary. Glass was often reshaped or flared after it was removed from the molds to give a larger variety of forms. The John B. Higbee Glass Co. frequently did this. The mug diameter is given at the very top. Diameters and heights are rounded to the nearest 1/8 inch. Where cups and saucers are listed, only the cup size is given.

The English glass makers started using Trade Marks and Registry Numbers in 1842. These were to protect the designs from being reproduced, but they were not required.

Flint glass (containing lead) was used in making pressed glass at all factories in the United States until about 1863 when the soda-lime formula was perfected. Flint glass usually has a metallic ring when struck, however, this is not always the case. Some shapes do not transmit a bell tone resonance. The chemical formula from batch to batch often varied, causing some items to be less resonant. The last factories making pressed flint glass in the United States were the New England Glass Co. and the Boston & Sandwich Glass Co. They had stopped using it by 1875. Flint glass was used in England and Europe until the 1890s. Designs with animals, people, and plants made in flint glass are almost certainly made there.

Prices are a matter of supply and demand, and they may vary widely depending on the area of the country and the availability in that region, the number of collectors who are competing for a form or a pattern, and how much the dealer had to pay. We have tried to give fair and objective pricing by consulting numerous dealers in pattern glass and weighing their suggestions versus our own experiences. Remember that damage and sun discoloration severely reduce the value of the glass. Examine a possible acquisition carefully before you purchase it.

INTRODUCTION

A mug is a drinking container with a handle. Mugs have been made of many materials in a variety of shapes and sizes.

The primary emphasis of this book is early pattern glass mugs. The starting date for this book is after the first invention of methods for making pattern glass in 1825. The first commercial mugs of this type of glass date from the 1830s. The end of this period falls about 1930 with the closing of many glass factories due to the Great Depression. During the Great Depression, the glass designs and the colors were substantially different than those that were made earlier.

Some of the first pattern glass mugs that were made were whiskey tumblers with applied handles. About the same time pressed handle shot glasses or lemonades, that have been called "whiskey tasters" were manufactured. Steins, which were Germanic in origin, were made primarily for the drinking of heady brews and are shown in several early catalogs. A toddy is another drink for which special mugs were made. Later, mugs were produced for children as presents or rewards, and these often had fanciful designs in bright colors. Toy mugs were also made for children to play with. Mugs were often manufactured to remind one of a special person, place, occasion or event.

It is difficult to determine what should be included and collected as a mug. Items that are on the borderline are custard cups, cup and saucer sets, punch cups and some mustard containers. A collection should have boundaries. These are established by the room available for a proper display, by the funds available for acquisitions, and, above all, what excites you.

Space has been allotted at the end of the book to cover Art Glass mugs, later historic mugs and non-glass historic mugs.

Pattern glass mugs make an ideal collection. Some are easily found and inexpensive, while others are quite rare and very expensive. There's something for everyone from historic to humorous and plain to gaudy. Mugs are small enough to be easily displayed. A colored mug display in a sunny window is magnificent. However, be advised that clear glass will turn purple or yellow in direct sunlight over a period of time. This can undermine the value of an otherwise desirable mug.

Some mugs discussed in this book are not pictured. You might ask, "If you don't have a picture or haven't seen the mug, how can you be sure there was one?" I believe many patterns with tumblers and/or egg cups probably had workers apply handles to them to make a mug. These were not necessarily part of standard production. To include a mug as part of a pattern in this book, one or more reliable reference sources must list a mug having been made.

1

2

PEOPLE

1. **ALPHABET & CHILDREN (A.B.C.D.)**
2 1/4" dia. x 2 3/4" ht.
This mug was made by Adams & Co. in the 1880s and by the U. S. Glass Co. after 1891. One side has a girl decorating a Christmas tree and the other has a boy seated at a desk. The front has the alphabet. This mug is especially sought after by Christmas collectors. It was made in clear, amber, blue, green and opaque blue. The mug is rare in color.
Clear $70-90, Amber $130-150, Blue and Green $150-200, Opaque Blue $200-250
Ref.- GCF1 p. 90, HCT p. 106 (advertisement), PG&B p. 18 (advertisement), TOY p. 142

3

4

2. **BOY & GIRL FACE**
2 1/2" dia. x 2 5/8" ht.
The Columbia Glass Co. of Findlay, Ohio, manufactured this cup and saucer in the late 1880s. After 1891, it was made by the U. S. Glass Co. The cup has a boy's face surrounded by a wreath on one side and a girl's face surrounded by a wreath on the other. The saucer (called Acorn) has scrolled vines with oak leaves and acorns. One variation of the cup has a truncated cone added to the foot. It was made in clear, amber and blue.
Clear $50-60, Color $80-90, 50% less without saucer
Ref.- FIN p. 41 and 55, FINP p. 55, GCF1 p. 51, TOY p. 133

5

6

3. **BOY WITH BEGGING DOG**
3" dia. x 3 3/8" ht.
This mug was probably produced in the

7

8

9

1890s. It was made in clear, blue, opaque white and opaque blue. The mug is probably a companion piece to Deer & Cow and Heron & Peacock because the bowl and handle shapes are similar. The three mugs make a graduated size grouping.
Clear $45-55 Old Colors $65-75
Ref.- GCF1 p. 81, GCF2 p. 187, OPA plate 82, TOY p. 139

4. **BY JINGO**
$2^1/_4$" dia. x $2^1/_2$" ht. or $2^3/_4$" dia. x $2^7/_8$" ht. or 3 1/8" dia. x 3 3/8" ht.
This mug was made about 1880. It has a decorative band at the top. There is a man with hat sitting with his legs crossed on a bench with a shoe off (only on one side). Below him it reads, "BY JINGO". The front has a notched oval medallion. It was made in clear, amber and blue.
All Sizes in Clear $45-55
All Sizes in Colors $70-85
Ref.- GCF1 p. 86, MET2 p. 207, TOY p. 141

5. **MEDALLION (CERES)**
2" dia. x 2" ht. or $2^1/_2$" dia. x $2^1/_2$" ht. or $3^1/_8$" dia. x $3^1/_4$" ht.
Atterbury & Co. manufactured this mug and this pattern about 1870. The large mug's mold has been remade at least once. One variation is called Washington & Lafayette (compare the hair and the base of the bust). Ceres mugs were made in clear, amber, blue, opaque turquoise, opaque black, opaque raspberry, dark amethyst, opalescent, blue opalescent, blue alabaster and pink alabaster. Over 20 different items were made in this pattern.
All Colors and Sizes $30-55
Ref.- GCD, GCF1 p. 87, JLPG p. 140, MG p. 127 (advertisement), MMPG p. 368, PG&B p. 43, PITT p. 401 (advertisement), WHPG p. 64

6. **INDOOR DRINKING SCENE**
$2^7/_8$" dia. x 5" ht. or $5^3/_4$" ht.
The National Glass Co. (at the Indiana Tumbler & Goblet Works) was the maker of this mug about 1900-1903, and it is also shown in a 1907-08 Indiana Glass Co. catalogue. It was made in clear, chocolate and nile green.
Both Sizes Color $100-125
Ref.- GRE p. 78, GREE plate 275

7. **GRUMPY WOMAN & MAN (CAPTAIN HOOK)**
$1^7/_8$" dia. x 2" ht.
This toy mug was probably made in the 1880s. It has a man with a mustache on one side and an angry woman on the other. It is known in clear, frosted, opalescent and opaque blue.
Clear and Frosted $35-40
Opalescent $65-75
Opaque Blue $100-125
Ref.- TOY p. 138

8. **OUTDOOR DRINKING SCENE**
$2^7/_8$" dia. x 5" ht.
The National Glass Co. (at the Indiana Tumbler & Goblet Works) was the maker of this mug about 1902. It was shown in a 1907-08 Indiana Glass Co. catalogue. There are several mold variations, including a plain handle. It was made in clear, blue, chocolate and nile green.
Chocolate $100-125
Blue and Green $125-165
Ref.- GRE p. 78, GREE plate 275

9. **TROUBADOUR**
$2^3/_4$" dia. x $4^3/_4$" ht. or 5" ht. or $^1/_2$ gallon
The National Glass Co. (at the Indiana Tumbler & Goblet Co. factory) and McKee & Brothers were the makers of this mug about 1900. National made it in amber, chocolate, blue and nile green. Any other colors were made by McKee.
Chocolate and Blue $100-125
Nile Green $150-200 Other Colors $50-75 add 200% for ½ Gallon
Ref.- GRE p. 88, GREE plate 275

10. **CUPID & VENUS**
$1^7/_8$" dia. x $2^1/_8$" ht. or $2^1/_2$" dia. x $2^1/_2$" ht. or $3^1/_8$" dia. x $3^3/_8$" ht.
This pattern was made by the Richards & Hartley Flint Glass Co. about 1880 and after 1891 the U. S. Glass Co. continued production. The pattern was produced primarily in clear with a few pieces in canary and amber. The mugs were made only in clear. About 35 different pieces were made in this pattern.
All Sizes $35-50
Ref.- GCF1 p. 93, JLPG p. 140, LEE p. 360, TOY p. 153

11. **BATON WITH HANDS**
2 1/4" dia. x 4 3/8" ht.
This unusual mug has a handle that consists of 2 hands holding a baton that has balls at both ends. The bowl is plain with etching. The mug is known only in clear and is rare. It was probably made in the 1880s. This design is similar to the handle design on the pattern Cottage.
Clear $50-60
Ref.- None

10

14

12. **HUMPTY DUMPTY**
$2^7/_8$" dia. x $3^1/_2$" ht.
This mug was probably made in the 1880s in clear only. One side has Humpty Dumpty and the other Tom Tom the Piper's Son. It is believed to have been made in pink, amber, blue and green in the 1930s. A bowl, a tumbler, and plate in matching colors were also made.
All Colors $20-25
Ref.- GCF1 p. 85, MET2 p. 203, WHPG p. 148

13. **VIKING (BEARDED MAN)**
3" dia. x $3^3/_8$" ht.
This pattern was made Hobbs, Brockunier & Co. about 1876. A handle was added to the tumbler to make this scarce mug. It is rare when a notched cover is added to make it a mustard. The pattern was made in clear, is rare in opaque white and is scarce frosted. Some of the frosted pieces have only the man's head frosted, while others have the whole surface frosted, except for clear circles with frosted flowers. The mug is known only in clear. There are about 25 different items in the pattern.
Clear $100-125 add 50% for cover
Ref.- JLPG p. 543, MMPG p. 370, WHPG p. 37

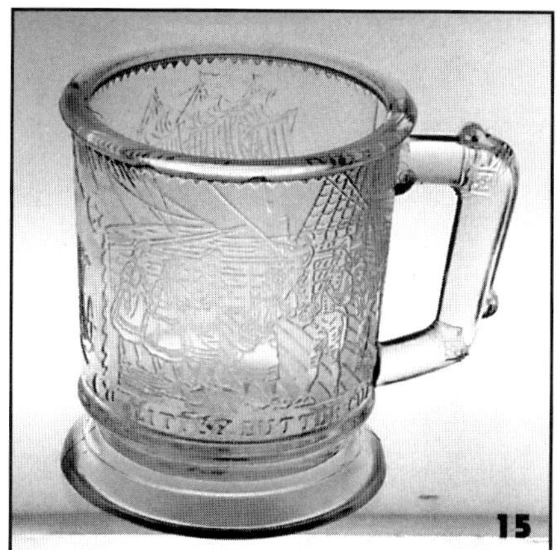

14. **SANTA & CHIMNEY**

3" dia. x 3 3/8" ht.

Dithridge & Co. made this mug about 1879. One side reads "EXAMINING HIS RECORDS" and shows Santa going down at chimney, while the other shows Santa in his sleigh. This mug is avidly sought by Christmas collectors. It was made only in clear. The unusual molded surface treatment on this mug is called "Crystalography". See Little Bo-Peep for more information.

Clear $225-275

Ref.- GCF1 p. 76, TOY p. 149

15. **LITTLE BUTTERCUP**

3 1/8" dia. x 3 1/2" ht.

Dithridge & Co. made this mug about 1879. One side says "LITTLE BUTTERCUP" and shows several girls and crew members standing on a ship deck. The other side says "H. M. S. PINAFORE" and shows a ship. The front shows an anchor and a capstan in a shield. It was made only in clear. The mug was made to commerorate the Gilbert & Sullivan operetta, "H.M.S. Pinafore" which was first performed in 1878. The unusual molded surface treatment on this mug is called "Crystalography". See Little Bo-Peep for more information.

Clear $60-80

Ref.- GCF1 p. 75, JLPG p. 4, MET2 p. 205, PITT p. 357, TOY p. 150

16. **LITTLE RED RIDING HOOD**

3" dia. x 3 3/8" ht.

Dithridge & Co. made this mug about 1879. One side says "LITTLE RED RIDINGHOOD" and shows "Red" and the wolf, while the other says "THE PARTING" and shows "Red" and Grandma in front of Grandma's house. It was made in clear only. The unusual molded surface treatment on this mug is called "Crystalography". See Little Bo-Peep for more information.

Clear $60-80

Ref.- TOY p. 150

17. **LITTLE BO-PEEP**

3 1/8" dia. x 3 1/2" ht.

Dithridge & Co. showed this mug in an 1879 advertisement for this type surface treatment. One side says "LITTLE BO-PEEP" and has a girl and a dog, while the other says "HAS LOST HER SHEEP" and shows several sheep. It was made in clear only. The unusual molded surface treatment on this mug is called "Crystalography". A patent was granted to lithographer Henry Feurhake in 1879 and assigned to mold maker Washington Beck for this process. Feurhake said, "The distinguishing characteristic is a fine granular surface, which partially obscures and partially reflects light, whereby a new and peculiar effect is produced." This process was meant to replace the more labor intensive manufacturing methods of acid frosting and etching by creating a similar effect in the mold.

Clear $70-90

Ref.- GCF1 p.75, PITT p.357, TOY p.149

18. **LITTLE BO-PEEP VARIANT**
3 1/8"dia. x 3 1/2"ht.
This mug is the same as Little Bo-Peep, except it has a lamb on the base.
Clear $100-125
Ref.- GCF1 p.86, TOY p.153

19. **DOG & CHILD**
not shown
The National Glass Co. at the Indiana Tumbler & Goblet Works was the maker of this mug about 1900-1903. It was made in clear, chocolate and nile green.
Clear $100-125
Chocolate $200-250
Nile Green $250-300
Ref.- GRE fig.172, WHPG p. 96

20. **MERCURY**
2 1/4"dia. x 3"ht.
This flint mug was probably made in England or Europe in the 1880s. There is a basket of flowers on each side with a stippled background and a bust of Mercury is in a circle on the front. It's known only in light green.
Light Green $60-75
Ref.- None

21. **CUPID IN ARCH**
3"dia. x 3 3/8" ht.
This opaque white mug was probably made in the early 1900s. Because of the similarity in design, this was possibly made by the same manufacturer as Rose Panels.
Opaque White $45-55
Ref.- None

22. **OUR BOY / JESTER ON PIG**
3 1/8" dia. x 3 3/8" ht.
McKee & Brothers probably made this mug about 1887. A jester riding a pig backward is shown on one side and the words "Our Boy" are on the other. It was made in clear, amber, blue, canary and apple green. It is probably a companion piece to Our Girl / Little Bo-Peep.
Clear $40-50 Amber $65-75
Other Color $75-95
Ref.- MET2 p. 207

23. **OUR GIRL / LITTLE BO-PEEP**
3 1/8"dia. x 3 3/8" ht.
McKee & Brothers made this mug about 1887. A girl and a lamb are shown on one side and the words "Our Girl" are on the other. It was made in clear, amber, blue, canary and apple green. It is probably a companion piece to Our Boy / Jester on Pig.
Clear $40-50 Amber $65-75
Other Color $75-95
Ref.- GCF1 p. 75, GR1, TOY p. 151

24. **TREE CLIMBER**
2 3/8" dia. x 2 1/2" ht.
This mug was probably made in the 1890s. One side has a boy climbing a tree to get away from a dog that's pulling at his pants. The other side has a Santa's head sticking out of a chimney. This mug should attract Christmas collectors. It is known only in opaque white and probably had painted decoration.
Opaque White $50-60
add 50% for good paint
Ref.- TOY p. 141

25. **LITTLE BO-PEEP, WESTMORELAND'S**
3 1/8" dia. x 3"ht.
The Westmoreland Specialty Co. made this mug in the 1920s. There is a matching plate. It was made in clear, frosted, marigold carnival, clear with white and blue decoration, opaque blue and red-orange clambroth.
Clear and Paint $50-60
Color $70-90 Carnival $150-200
Ref.- CARN p. 29, GCF1 p. 86, HGC5 p. 38, TOY p. 153

26. **MONK & STEIN**
1 1/2" dia. x 2" ht. or 2 1/4" dia. x 4" ht.
This stein was probably made about 1900. It has a monk holding a stein with a raised cover on each side. It was made in clear and opaque white and was probably painted.
Small $25-30 Large $35-45
add 25% for good paint
Ref.- GCF1 p. 75, TOY p. 113

27. **MONK**
1 3/8" dia. x 2" ht.
The U. S. Glass Co. made these steins about 1900. They were made in clear and opaque white, and the latter was often painted pink and gold.
Clear $20-25 Opaque White $35-45
add 25% for good paint
Ref.- None

28. **PUNCH & JUDY**
3 1/4"dia. x 4" ht.
This opaque white mug has Punch on one side and Judy on the other. It was probably made in England or France in the 1880s.
Opaque White $100-125
Ref.- MG p. 49

20

21

24

22

25

23

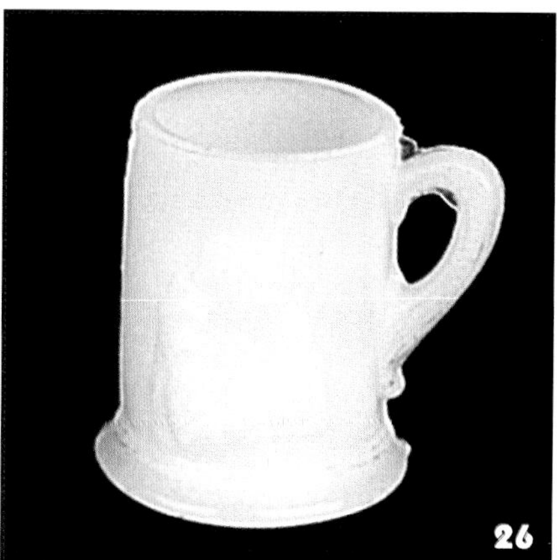
26

27

28

ANIMALS

29

30

31

32

33

29. **MONKEY & VINES**
2 1/2" dia. x 2 1/2" ht.
Dithridge & Co. made this mug about 1879. One side has a monkey looking at a turtle with a question mark, while the other has the turtle biting the monkey's finger with an exclamation point. It was only produced in clear. The unusual molded surface treatment on this and other similar mugs is called "Crystalography". See Little Bo-Peep for more information.
Clear $45-55
Ref.- GCF1 p. 76, TOY p. 148

30. **SQUIRREL**
2 1/8" dia. x 3"
Adams & Co. made this mug in the 1880s. After 1891, it was made by the U. S. Glass Co. It was manufactured in clear, is rare in blue and opaque blue.
Clear $30-40 Color $75-100
Ref.- GCF1 p. 79, TOY p. 142

31. **CAT IN A HAT**
2 1/2" dia. x 2 1/2" ht.
This mug was probably manufactured at the turn of the century. It was made in clear, opaque white with yellow and green paint, and opaque blue.
Clear $65-75 Color $80-100
Ref.- GCF1 p. 77, TOY p. 148

32. **FIGHTING CATS**
1 7/8" dia. x 2 1/8" ht.
Dithridge & Co. made this mug about 1879. One side has 2 cats hissing at each other on a fence, while the other side has 2 fighting cats with their tails tied together and thrown over a clothesline. It was only produced in clear. The unusual molded surface treatment on this mug is called "Crystalography". See Little Bo-Peep for more information.
Clear $45-55
Ref.- GCF1 p. 79, MET2 p. 203, TOY p. 150

33. **CAT IN A TANGLE**
1 3/4" dia. x 2" ht.
The 1880s is most likely when this mug was produced. It shows a cat trapped in flowers and plants. It was made in clear and amber.
Clear $50-60 Amber $70-90
Ref.- GCF1 p. 77, TOY p. 143

34. **DOG MEDALLION**
1 3/4" ht. not shown
This cup and saucer was probably made in the 1880. It is known in clear and possibly blue.
Clear $100-125
without saucer 50% less
Ref.- GCF1 p. 50, MET2 p. 217, PP1 p. 23 TOY p. 133

35. **ELEPHANT, HEISEY'S (FAIRY TALES)**
3" dia. x 3" ht. not shown
The A. C. Heisey Co. made this mug. It has eight panels with a picture to represent a different story on each one. It was only produced in clear and was marked with the Heisey trademark, "H" inside a diamond. It was reproduced in color in a different mold by the Imperial Glass Co.
Old Clear $300-350
Ref.- GCF2 p.

36. **WESTWARD HO (PIONEER)**
2" ht. or 2 1/4" dia. x 2 3/4" ht. or 2 7/8" dia. x 3 1/2" ht.
Gillinder & Sons were the makers of this pattern about 1879. It was produced in clear and acid frosted. The mugs were also made in opalescent, opaque white, blue and opaque blue. These are especially rare in color. Many items in this pattern have been reproduced, but the mug has not. There is a stag on one side and an American bison on the other. The amount of background detail decreases as the size decreases.
All Sizes Clear $200-250
All Sizes Opalescent and Opaque White $400-550
All Sizes Blue and Opaque Blue $500-650
Ref.- GCF1 p. 77, JLPG p. 552, LEE p. 285

37. **BABY ANIMALS**
2 1/2" dia. x 2 3/4" ht. or
3 1/8"dia. x 3 1/8" ht.
A cat in a basket and bear on a drum are shown on this mug. The large size has a flower in the base. It was probably made in the 1890s. It was made in clear and colors. The small size was reproduced in color by the Mosser Glass Co. and in carnival for the Lincoln Land Carnival Club as a souvenir in 1977. Colors that are not typical of this era are reproductions.
Old, Both Sizes $30-40
Ref.- GCF1 p. 74, TOY p. 143

38. **DEER & OAK TREE**
2 3/8"dia. x 3 1/8" ht.
The National Glass Co. at the Indiana Tumbler & Goblet Works was the maker of this mug about 1900-1903. It was made in clear and chocolate.
Clear $50-60 Chocolate $200-250
Ref.- GRE fig.171, TOY p. 137

39. **GARDEN OF EDEN (LOTUS & SERPENT)**
3" dia. x 3 5/8"ht.
This pattern was manufactured about 1880 possibly by McKee & Brothers. Some items in this pattern have the serpent, while others do not. The mug has the serpent, which looks somewhat like the head of a turtle. Over 20 different pieces were made in this pattern. It was made in clear only.
Clear $35-40
Ref.- GCF1 p. 90, JLPG p. 240, MET2 p. 205

40. **RABBIT, SITTING**
3 1/8" dia. x 3 3/8"ht.
The Central Glass Co. made this mug in the 1880s. After 1891, it was made by the U. S. Glass Co. The rabbit is sitting on one side and running on the other. One has a plain bottom, while the other has a rayed bottom. It was made in clear and amber.
Clear $55-65 Amber $80-100 *Ref.- HC5 p. 91 (advertisement), PG&B p. 113 (advertisement), TOY p. 147*

41. **RABBIT, SITTING VARIANT**
3" dia. x 3 1/2" ht.
The Challinor, Taylor & Co. Ltd. manufactured this mug in the 1880s. This mug is the same as the one listed above, except there are 2 mold variations - one has a lamb on the bottom and the slag has a rayed base. It was known in clear and purple slag.
Clear $90-110 Purple Slag $100-125
Ref.- TAR p. 51

42. **LAMB**
2 3/4" dia. x 3" ht.
The Iowa City Glass Co. may have made this mug about 1881. The shape of the bowl and the handle is the same as House & Boat Medallion and very similar to Dog with Collar. It was made in clear, blue, dark turquoise and dark amethyst.
Clear $55-65 Color $100-125
Ref.- GCF1 p. 92, TOY p. 147

43. **DOG WITH COLLAR**
3 1/8" dia. x 3 3/8" ht.
The Iowa City Glass Co. manufactured this mug about 1881. It was made in clear and amethyst. The mold has been remade at least once. In the other version, the dog does not have a collar.
Clear $55-65 Amethyst $100-125
Ref.- IOW p. 43

44. **BEGGING DOG**
2" dia. x 2 3/8" ht.
This mug was probably manufactured by the Iowa City Glass Co. about 1881. The handle and the bowl shape are the same as Dog with Collar. It was made in clear, amethyst and perhaps cobalt.
Clear $45-55 Color $80-100
Ref.- GCF1 p. 81, TOY p. 142

36 front

36 back

42

43

44

45

46

47

48

49

50

51

52

53

54 front

54 back

55

56

57

58

45. **DEER & COW**
1 7/8" dia. x 2" ht.
This mug was probably made in the 1880s. It was manufactured in clear, blue, opaque white and opaque blue. The mug is likely a companion piece to Heron & Peacock and Boy with Begging Dog because the bowl and handle shapes are similar. This is the smallest mug in the graduated grouping.
Clear $30-40 Opaque White $40-50 Color $50-60
Ref.- TOY p. 145, PP2 p. 85

46. **DEER & PINETREE**
2 3/8" dia. x 2 3/8" ht. or 2 3/4" dia. x 2 3/4" ht. or 3" dia. x 3 1/4" ht.
McKee & Brothers made this pattern about 1886. It is possible that the Belmont Glass Co. also made it. The mugs were manufactured in clear, amber, dark amber, blue, emerald green, yellow-green, apple green and with gold. Over 25 different pieces were made in this pattern.
All Colors and Sizes $45-70
Ref.- GCF1 p. 78, HGC1 p. 3 (advertisement), JLPG p. 169, MMPG p. 14, TOY p. 145

47. **DOG CHASING DEER**
3 1/4" dia. x 3 3/4" ht.
Bryce Brothers made this mug in the 1880s. After 1891, it was manufactured by the U. S. Glass Co. It was made in clear, frosted, amber, opaque white, and blue. This is the largest mug in a graduated 4 piece set. The other mugs are Swan, Pointing Dog and Bird on a Branch.
Frosted and Clear $40-50
Amber and Opaque White $55-65
Blue $60-75
Ref.- GCF1 p. 80, HC5 p. 86 (advertisement), PG&B p. 90 (advertisement), TOY p. 139

48. **POINTING DOG**
2 3/8" dia. x 2 5/8" ht.
Bryce Brothers made this mug in the 1880s. The U. S. Glass Co. continued production after 1891. It was manufactured in clear, frosted, amber, opaque white, and blue. This is the third largest mug in a graduated 4 piece set. The others are Swan, Bird on a Branch and Dog Chasing Deer.
Frosted and Clear $35-40
Amber and Opaque White $50-60
Blue $55-65
Ref.- GCF1 p. 80, HC5 p. 86 (advertisement), PG&B p. 90 (advertisement), TOY p. 139

49. **FEEDING DEER & DOG**
2 3/8" dia. x 2 5/8" ht.
Bryce Brothers made this mug in the 1880s. After 1891, it was made by the U. S. Glass Co. It was produced in clear, amber, blue, canary and light amethyst. It is the next to the smallest size mug in a gradauted 4 mug set. The other mugs are Chick & Pugs, Grape Bunch and Robin in Tree. Strawberry & Pear has the same bowl and handle shape.
Clear $35-45 Colors $50-70
Ref.- GCF1 p. 79, HC5 p. 81 (advertisement), MET2 p. 203, TOY p. 137

50. **CAT ON A CUSHION (CAT & DOG)**
2 1/8" dia. x 2 1/8" ht.
The Columbia Glass Co. probably produced this cup and saucer in the late 1880s. The U. S. Glass Co. made it after 1891. The cup has a cat in a basket on one side, while the other has a dog running in front of a picket fence. The saucer has a pair of boots with a cat in one. The cup and saucer was made in clear, amber and blue.
Clear $75-95 Color $110-135 50% less without saucer
Ref.- GCF2 p. 51, CORN p. 168 (saucer), HC5 p. 179 (advertisement), TOY p. 133

51. **RABBIT, UPRIGHT**
3 1/8" dia. x 3 1/4" ht.
This pattern was most likely produced in the 1880s. It was made in clear, amber, blue, apple green and possibly canary. It is a probably a companion piece to Wolf and possibly Diamond with Circle.
Clear and Amber $50-60 Blue and Apple Green $65-80
Ref.- GCF1 p. 78, TOY p. 147

52. **FISHERMAN**
2 3/4" dia. x 4" ht.
The Dugan Glass Co. and its successor, the Diamond Glass-Ware Co., made this mug between 1911 and 1914. It was produced only in carnival colors. These are marigold, amethyst, horehound, blue and peach opalescent.
Amethyst $100-120 Marigold and Horehound $225-275 Blue $300-350 Peach Opal .$1200+
Ref.- CARN p. 79, HCP2 p. 19 (advertisement)

53. **WOLF**
3 3/4" dia. x 3 3/4" ht.
This pattern was probably made in the 1880s. It was produced in clear, amber, blue, apple green and maybe in canary. It is a likely a companion piece to Wolf and possibly Diamond with Circle.
Clear and Amber $60-70 Blue and Apple Green $75-100
Ref.- GCF1 p. 78, TOY p. 146

54. **LION HUNT**
4" dia. x 5 1/4" ht.
This mug was probably made in the 1880s. This amber specimen is very rare. This mug shows an Arab or an Indian hunter shooting a charging lion. They are surrounded by tropical foliage, rocks, and palm trees. There are 15 panels on the mug. This is probably a companion piece to the Shrine, Lion with Flag Mug.
Amber $225-275
Ref.- None

55. **DOG & QUAIL**
2 7/8" dia. x 3 1/4" ht.
This mug was made by the Paden City Glass Manufacturing Co. about 1916. It is shown in one of their catalogues. The mold has been remade at least once. One version has the dog to the right of the handle, while the other has the dog to the left. It was made in clear and amber.
Clear $55-65 Amber $75-95
Ref.- GCF1 p. 77, PC p. 79 (advertisement), TOY p. 146

56. **ELEPHANT**
3 1/8" dia. x 3 5/8" ht.
This rare mug was manufactured by the Central Glass Co. After 1891, it was made by the U. S. Glass Co. It was produced in clear, amber and blue. The mug is very rare in blue. This is not part of the Jumbo pattern.
Clear $125-175 Amber $200-250 Blue $275-325
Ref.- PG&B p. 113 (advertisement), TOY p. 156 (advertisement)

57. **METAMORPHOSIS**
3 1/8" dia. x 3 3/8" ht.
This flint mug is probably English or European from the 1880s. It has a goat's head (?) turning into a wolf with claws in foliage. The handle is a goose's head and neck. It was made in clear, frosted, opaque white and opaque blue.
Clear and Frosted $90-110
Color $125-150
Ref.- None

59

60

61

58. **SNAKE IN THE ORCHARD**
3 1/4" dia. x 3 7/8" ht.
This mug may truly be called Garden of Eden, however, that name is already in use and is well known. There are cherries and peaches with foliage on a stippled background. There are decorative bands at the top and bottom and, of course, the snake handle. It is amber and very rare.
Amber $150-200
Ref.- None

59. **MONKEY w/ FANCY HANDLE**
3 1/8" dia. x 3 3/8" ht.
The Valley Glass Co. made this mug about 1891. It is not part of the Duncan's "Monkey" pattern, although the design is very similar. It was part of the Darwin Line that was advertised in a July 17, 1890 trade journal. It was made in clear, amethyst, and possibly in pale blue.
Clear $90-110 Amethyst $175-225
Ref.- GCF1 p. 76, JLPG p. 374, LEE p. 319, TOY p. 137

60. **MONKEY w/ DIAMOND BASE**
3 1/8" dia. x 3 5/8" ht.
This mug was probably manufactured in the 1880s. This mug is not part of the Monkey pattern. It was made only in clear.
Clear $90—110
Ref.- JLPG p. 374, LEE p. 319, MET2 p. 207, MMPG p. 16, TOY p. 136

61. **KITTEN**
The Challinor, Taylor & Co. Ltd. made this mug in the 1880s. The U.S. Glass Co. took over production in 1891. It was produced in clear and possibly other colors.
Clear $40-50
Ref.- HC5 p. 91 (advertisement), TAR p. 51

62. **LION**
not shown
This toy pattern was probably made by Gillinder & Sons about 18 The item listed here is a cup and saucer. There is also a miniature 4 piece table set. It was made in clear, acid frosted and rare opaque blue.
Clear and Frosted $100-125
Opaque Blue $200-250 without saucer 50% less
Ref.- CORN p. 167, GCF1 p. 50, MET2 p. 217, TOY p. 133

BIRDS AND INSECTS

63

64

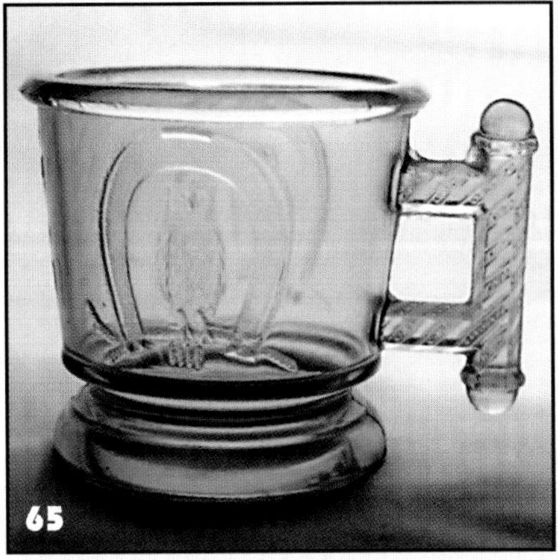
65

63. **ROBIN, ATTERBURY'S (EASTLAKE)**
shaving mug: 3 5/8" dia. x 3 3/8" ht. or mug: 1 7/8" dia. x 2" ht. or 2 1/2" dia. x 2 5/8" ht. or 3 1/4" dia. x 3 3/8" ht. or 3 1/2" dia. x 4" ht.
Atterbury & Co. made these mugs about 1880. There is a variation of the 3 1/4" dia. mug that doesn't have foliage on the front. This is probably a remake of the mold. This mug has the same handle as Owl & Horseshoe. They were produced in clear, amber, blue, blue alabaster, opaque white, opaque black, amethyst alabaster, pink alabaster, opaque raspberry and blue opalescent.
All Sizes in Clear $30-40
All Sizes in Colors $ 40-55
Ref.- GCD1, GCD2, MG p. 127 (advertisement), TOY p. 144

64. **HERON & PEACOCK**
2 1/2" dia. x 2 5/8" ht.
This mug was originally manufactured in the late 1800s. It was made in clear, blue, opaque white and opaque blue. It has been heavily reproduced. Early reproductions by Degenhart have a "D" inside a heart trademark. Many reproductions were made later in other colors. It is probably a companion piece to Deer & Cow and Boy with Begging Dog because of the bowl and handle shape.
Clear $25-30 Colors $30-40
Ref.- GCF1 p. 81, MET2 p. 207, TOY p. 144

65. **OWL & HORSESHOE**
3 3/8" dia. x 3 1/8" ht.
This pattern was probably by Atterbury & Co. in the 1880s. Atterbury is the only factory known to make this color range. This mug has the same handle as Atterbury's Robin. There is no connection between this mug and the goblet shown in Metz I. This mug was made in clear, amber, blue, pink clambroth, opaque white and possibly other colors.
Clear $35-45 Colors $45-60
Ref.- GCD, MG p. 45

66. **BIRDS & INSECTS**
3 5/8" dia. x 4 1/8" ht.
This mug was made about 1880 in clear and amber. It has seven birds and two insects. There is also a goblet.
Clear $60-70 Amber $90-110
Ref.- None

67. **STORK & RUSHES VARIANT**
2 7/8" dia. x 3 7/8" ht.
The Dugan Glass Co. and its successor, the Diamond Glass-Ware Co., made this pattern from about 1910 to 1915. Stork & Rushes has beaded bands, whereas, this pattern has lattice bands. It was produced in the carnival colors: marigold, amethyst and blue.
Marigold $35-45 Amethyst $65-75
Blue $325-375
Ref.- HCG2 p. 72 (advertisement), HGC5 p. 46 (advertisement), MMPG p. 26

68. **BIRD ON A BRANCH**
2 7/8" dia. x 3 3/8" ht.
Bryce Brothers made this mug in the 1880s. The U. S. Glass Co. made it after 1891. It was produced in clear, frosted, opaque white, amber and blue. This is the second largest mug in a graduated 4 piece set. The other mugs are Swan, Pointing Dog and Dog Chasing Deer.
Frosted and Clear $35-45
Opaque White and Amber $40-50
Blue $45-55
Ref.- GCF1 p. 80, HC5 p. 86 (advertisement), KM7 p. 102 (advertisement), PG&B p. 90 (advertisement), TOY p. 139 and 146

69. **SWAN (WATER FOWL, U. S. GLASS' and FEDERAL'S NO. 3802)**
1 7/8" dia. x 2" ht.
Bryce Brothers manufactured this mug in the 1880s. After 1891, it was manufactured by the U. S. Glass Co. It is shown in a 1914 Federal Glass Company's Packer's Catalogue. This type glass was used to distribute condiments. It was made in clear, frosted, amber, opaque white and blue. This is the smallest mug in a graduated 4 piece set. The other mugs are Pointing Dog, Bird on a Branch and Dog Chasing Deer.
Clear $30-35 Color $35-50
Ref.- GCF1 p. 80, HC5 p. 86 (advertisement), HGC5 p. 40 (advertisement). PG&B p. 90 (advertisement), TOY p. 139 and 145

66

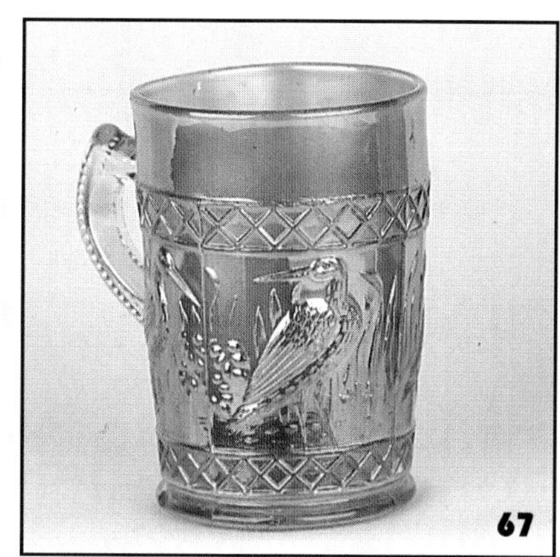
67

68

69

70

71

72

70. **ROBIN**
3 1/8" dia. x 3 1/2" ht.
The Imperial Glass Co. made this mug after 1910. It was produced in marigold carnival and smoke carnival.
Marigold $40-50 Smoke $100-125
Ref.- CARN p. 170

71. **SINGING BIRDS**
3 1/4" dia. x 3 1/2" ht.
The H. Northwood Co. of Wheeling, West Virginia, produced this pattern between 1911 and 1920. There are berry sets, water sets, table sets and a sherbet, as well as the mug. They are marked with the underlined "N" in a circle trademark. A rare amethyst carnival mug is known with advertising for the "Amazon Hotel & Cafe". It was made in many carnival colors: marigold, amethyst, blue, green, rare ice blue and rare aqua opalescent.
Marigold $125-150
Amethyst $90-110 Blue $200-250
Green $300-350
Aqua opalescent $1200-1500
Ice Blue $600-800
add 200% for advertising
Ref.- CARN p. 182, MMPG p. 26

72. **SINGING BIRDS, STIPPLED**
2 7/8" dia. x 3 7/8" ht.
This mug is similar to the one listed above, but obviously from a different mold. It is marked with the underlined "N" in a circle trademark. It was made in the carnival colors: marigold, amethyst, blue and light blue-green. Sometimes these are souvenired.
Ref.- None

73

74

75

76

78

79

73. **BIRD & HARP**
$2\,^1/_4$" dia. x $2\,^3/_8$" ht. or
$2\,^5/_8$"dia. x $2\,^3/_4$" ht. (bird flies to right)
or $3\,^1/_8$" dia. x $3\,^1/_8$" ht. (bird stands on nest facing left)
This mug was made by McKee & Brothers about 1880. There is a harp on each side of the handle. It was produced in clear and purple slag.
All Sizes Clear $30-40 All Sizes Purple Slag $60-80
Ref.- GCF1 p. 91, MET2 p. 207, MK p. 76 (advertisement), TOY p. 137, WHPG p. 42

74. **WHIRLING CHICKEN**
$2\,^3/_8$" dia. x 3" ht.
This mug was probably made in England or Europe in the 1880s. It is known only in clear.
Clear $35-40
Ref.- None

75. **SWAN & EGRET**
$1\,^7/_8$" dia. x $2\,^1/_8$" ht.
This mug was probably made in the 1880s. It has a swan on one side and an egret on the other. It is known only in clear.
Clear $35-40
Ref.- None

76. **BIRDS AT FOUNTAIN**
$1\,^3/_4$" dia. x $1\,^7/_8$" ht.
This mug was probably produced in the 1880s. There are 2 mold variations, one with the design on the front and the other with the design on both sides. It was made in clear, opaque white, alabaster and blue alabaster.
Clear $25-35 Colors $50-60
Ref.- GCF1 p. 81, TOY p. 145, WHPG p. 42

77. **BIRD IN NEST WITH FLOWERS**
not shown
$3\,^1/_8$" dia. x $3\,^3/_8$" ht.
Challinor & Taylor Ltd. manufactured this mug in the 1880s. It has a cat on the bottom. It was made in clear and purple slag.
Clear $55-65 Purple Slag $110-130
Ref.- None

78. **BIRD IN NEST WITH FLOWERS VARIANT**
$3\,^1/_8$" dia. x $3\,^3/_8$" ht.
This mug is the same as the one just listed, except it has a star on the bottom. It was made in clear and with paint.
Clear and Paint $35-45
Ref.- HC5 p. 91 (advertisement), TOY p. 136

79. **OWL ON A BRANCH**
$2\,^5/_8$" dia. x $3\,^3/_4$" ht.
This mug was probably manufactured by Dithridge & Co. about 1879. Each side has an owl on a branch with foliage. It was made only in clear. The unusual molded surface treatment on this mug is called "Crystalography". See Little Bo-Peep for more information.
Clear $35-45
Ref.- None

80

81

82

80. **HERON**
4" ht.
The Dugan Glass Co. and its successor, the Diamond Glass-Ware Co., made this mug between 1910 and 1914. It was produced only in carnival colors. These are amethyst and rare marigold.
Marigold $750-850
Amethyst $225-275
Ref.- CARN p. 102, HC2 p. 71

81. **HERON IN WEEDS**
1 7/8" dia. x 2" ht.
This mug was probably made in the 1890s. It is known only in opaque white, but probably had painted decoration.
Opaque White $35-45
add 25% for good paint.
Ref.- CARN p. 102, HC2 p. 71

82. **BUTTERFLY ON LOG**
2 3/8" dia. x 2" ht.
This could be a mug, a match holder or a toothpick and was probably made in the 1880s. It was produced in clear and with a frosted butterfly.
Clear and Frosted $45-50
Ref.- GCF1 p. 80, TOY p. 142

83. **CHICKS & PUGS**
1 7/8" dia. x 2" ht.
Bryce Brothers manufactured this mug in the 1880s. After 1891, it was made by the U. S. Glass Co. It was produced in clear, amber, blue, canary, and amethyst. It is the smallest mug in a graduated 4 mug set. The other mugs are Feeding Deer & Dog, Grape Bunch and Robin in Tree. Strawberry & Pear has the same shape and handle.
Clear $35-45 Colors $50-65
Ref.- HC5 p. 81 (advertisement), GCF1 p. 79, TOY p. 143

84. **ROBIN IN TREE**
3 1/4" dia. x 3 3/4" ht.
Bryce Brothers manufactured this mug in the 1880s. The U. S. Glass Co. made it after 1891. A reproduction by Mosser Glass Co. has an "M" inside an outline of the state of Ohio trademark. It was produced in clear, amber, blue, canary and light amethyst. It is the largest mug in a 4 mug set. The other mugs are Chick & Pugs, Feeding Deer & Dog and Grape Bunch. Strawberry & Pear has the same shape and handle style.
Clear $30-40 Color $45-55
Ref.- TOY p. 136, HC5 p. 81 (advertisement)

85. **SWIMMING SWAN**
3 3/8" dia. x 3 5/8" ht.
Atterbury & Co. was probably the maker this mug in the 1880s. It was produced in amber, black, olive amber, turquoise, opalescent, alabaster, turquoise alabaster, olive amber opalescent and opaque off-white.
Color $40-60
Ref.- GCD, HCG1 p. 10

86. **SWIMMING SWAN VARIANT**
3 1/8" dia. x 3 3/8" ht.
Atterbury & Co. probably made this mug in the 1880s. It is extremely rare. It is known only in brown alabaster, however, it was probably made in the full range of Atterbury colors. This color has been seen on a medium size "Swan with Ring Handle" mug. Some experts say that attributions can't be made using color, but I think Atterbury is an exception to the rule.
Color $80-1000
Ref.- None

87. **SWAN WITH RING HANDLE**
1 7/8" dia. x 2 1/8" ht. or 2 3/8" dia. x 2 5/8" ht. or 3 1/8" dia. x 3 1/2"ht.
Atterbury & Co. probably manufactured these mugs in the 1880s, and they are the known only makers of this color range. Some mugs have 3 balls at the middle of the ring. They were made in clear, amber, blue, opaque white, opalescent, blue alabaster, brown alabaster, pink alabaster, amber alabaster, opaque black and others.
All Sizes in Clear $30-45 All Sizes in Color $40-60
Ref.- GCD1, GCF1 p. 78, TOY p. 140

88. **BUTTERFLY WITH SPRAY (ACME)**
2" dia. x 2" ht. or 2 1/2" dia. x 2 1/2" ht. or 2 3/4" ht. or 3 1/4" dia. x 3 1/4" ht.
These mugs were made by Bryce, Higbee & Co. about 1883. They were produced in clear, clear with a blue painted butterfly, amber, blue and canary.
All Sizes Clear $35-45 All Sizes Colors and Paint $45-65
Ref.- GCF1 p. 83, KM8 p. 130 (advertisement), MMPG p. 22, TOY p. 144, WHPG p. 55

83

84

85

86

87

88

PLANTS

89

90

91

92

93

94

89. **ACANTHUS LEAVES**
1 7/8" dia. x 2" ht.
Doyle & Co. is believed to be the maker because of similarities in the leaf design to Grape & Festoon with Shield, a known Doyle pattern, and the use of the same starch blue color. This mug was probably made in the 1870s. It was made in clear, blue and opaque white.
Clear and Opaque White $25-30
Blue $45-55
Ref.- GCF1 p. 91, MET1 p. 79, PAT p. 160

90. **CACTUS**
3" dia. x 3 3/8" ht.
This mug was made by the Indiana Tumbler & Goblet Co. at Greentown, Indiana, about 1901, and production continued after the plant was taken over by the National Glass Co.. The pattern was displayed at the Pan-American Exposition in Buffalo, New York, during the summer of 1901. Reproductions of various items in the pattern were made by the St. Clair Glass Co. and the Fenton Art Glass Co. The mug has been reproduced in chocolate.
Clear $45-55 Chocolate $70-90
Ref.- GRE p. 73, OPA plate 242, WHPG p. 58

91. **CURLED LEAF (VINE BAND, KING'S NO. 198)**
2" dia. x 2 3/8" ht. or 2 1/2" dia. x 2 7/8" ht. or 3" dia. x 3 1/2" ht.
These mugs were manufactured by King Glass Co. in the 1880s and after 1891, by the U. S. Glass Co. They were made in clear, cobalt, canary and light amethyst. Occassionally, the mug is seen with a mustard lid.
All Sizes in Clear $35-45 All Sizes in Colors $70-90
Ref.- HOB1, PG&B p. 217 (advertisement), MET1 p. 61, GCF1 p. 83

92. **DAISY BAND**
2 1/2" dia. x 2 5/8" ht.
This cup and saucer was probably made by the Columbia Glass Co. in the late 1880s and perhaps by the U. S. Glass Co. after 1891. It was made in clear, amber and blue.
Clear $45-55 Color $70-80 50% less without saucer
Ref.- GCF1 p. 51, TOY p. 133

93. **DIAMOND CUT WITH LEAF (LEAF & TRIANGLE)**
2 3/8" dia. x 2 3/8"ht. or 2 7/8" dia. x 2 7/8" ht. or 3 1/4" dia. x 3 1/4" ht.
This pattern was manufactured by the Windsor Glass Co. around 1890. It was produced in clear,light amber and blue. Other than the mug, there is a 4 piece table set, a goblet and a plate.
All Sizes Clear $35-45
All Sizes Color $50-60
Ref.- GCF1 p. 89, MMPG p. 400, WEPG p. 243

94. **POPPY**
2" dia. x 2 5/8" ht.
This mug was probably manufactured in England or Europe in the 1880s. It is known only in blue.
Blue $40-50
Ref.- None

95

96

97

98

99

100

95. **PANELLED APPLE BLOSSOMS / BABY**
$2\,^1/_2$" dia. x $3\,^3/_8$" ht.
This mug is similar to item #97, except that it bears the word "BABY" and the band at the top is skewed. The D. C. Jenkins Glass Co. probably was the maker about 1907. It was made only in clear.
Clear $25-30
Ref.- None

96. **BLACKBERRY SPRAY**
$3\,^3/_8$" dia. x $3\,^5/_8$" ht.
This mug is the same size and shape with the same style handle as the Orange Tree mug. It was probably manufactured by the Fenton Art Glass Co. around 1911. It was made in clear (perhaps with yellow and green paint), cobalt and custard, often with gold or silver berries.
Clear and Paint $25-30
Color $35-45
Ref.- None

97. **PANELLED APPLE BLOSSOMS / DARLING**
$2\,^1/_2$" dia. x $3\,^3/_8$" ht.
This mug is shown in a 1907 D. C. Jenkins Glass Co. catalogue. It was made only in clear. The word "DARLING" is on the mug.
Clear $25-30
Ref.- ALB p. 118,
JJ p. 49 (advertisement)

98. **PANELLED CHERRY / SWEETHEART**
$2\,^3/_8$" dia. x $3\,^3/_8$" ht.
The Kokomo Glass Mfg. Co. made this mug about 1904. It was only produced in clear. The mug is marked "SWEETHEART".
Clear $25-30
Ref.- ALB p. 116,
JJ p. 46 (advertisement)

99. **GRAPEVINE WITH THUMBPRINT BAND**
The D. C. Jenkins Glass Co. manufactured this mug about 1920. It was made in clear only.
Clear $25-35
Ref.- JJ p. 25 (advertisement)

100. **CHERRIES / SWEETHEART**
$2\,^3/_8$" dia. x $3\,^1/_4$" ht.
The D. C. Jenkins Glass Co. manufactured this mug about 1920. The word "SWEETHEART" curves around the base. It was made only in clear.
Clear $25-30
Ref.- FINP p. 116, GR3

101

102

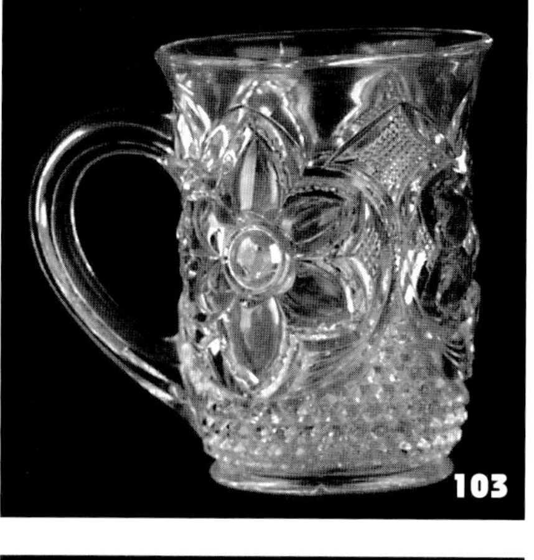
103

104

105

106

101. **GRAPE / DARLING**
The D. C. Jenkins Glass Co. started making this mug in 1907. It was made in clear only. "DARLING" is written on the bowl.
Clear $25-30
Ref.- FINP p. 119,
JJ p. 50 (advertisement)

102. **FLORAL OVAL**
2 7/8" dia. x 3 1/4" ht.
The J. B. Higbee Glass Co. made this pattern around 1910. After 1915 it was produced by the New Martinsville Glass Manufacturing Co. The pattern was produced only in clear. There are over 50 different pieces in this pattern.
Clear $25-30
Ref.- WHPG p. 115

103. **FLOWER WITH CANE (U. S. GLASS' NO. 15141)**
3" dia. x 3 5/8" ht.
The U. S. Glass Co. manufactured this mug about 1895. It was made in clear, clear with pink, amethyst or green flowers and with gold.
Clear $25-30 Stain $30-40
Ref.- MMPG p. 274 (mug not listed)

104. **PLAIN PETALS**
2 1/2" dia. x 3 3/4" ht.
This mug was probably made after the turn of the century. It was made only in clear.
Clear $10-15
Ref.- None

105. **CHERRY SPRIG**
2 1/2" dia. x 2 3/4" ht.
This mug is known only in clear.
Clear $35-45
Ref.- GCF2 p. 189

106. **DAISY PLEAT**
2 1/4" dia. x 2 1/2" ht. or 2 3/4" dia. x 3" ht. or 3" dia. x 3 1/2" ht.
This mug was probably manufactured in the 1880s and is known only in clear.
Clear $20-25
Ref.- GCF1 p. 88

107

108

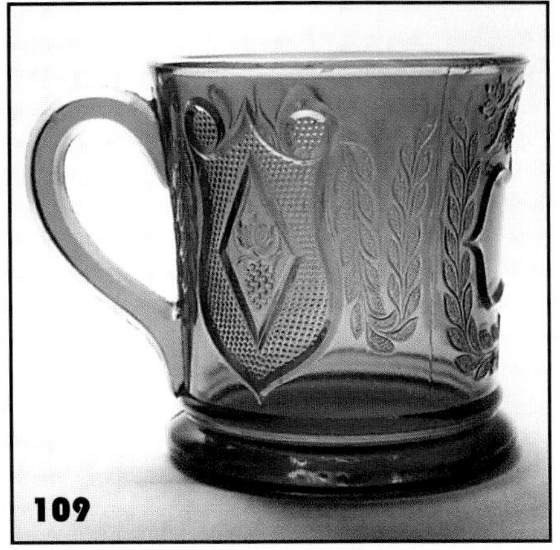
109

110

111

112

107. **GOOSEBERRY VARIANT**
$1^{7}/_{8}$" dia. x $1^{7}/_{8}$" ht.
Probably made in the 1880s, this mug was produced in clear, opaque white, blue, opaque blue and opaque teal.
Clear $20-25 Opaque Whire $25-30 Colors $30-40
Ref.- GCF1 p. 91, TOY p. 140

108. **FENTON ROSE**
$3^{1}/_{2}$" dia. x $3^{1}/_{2}$" ht.
The Fenton Art Glass Co. probably made this mug about 1920. It is similar in design and color to Fenton's Waterlily & Cattails, and the mug shape is the same as Orange Tree and Blackberry Spray. It was made in white opalescent, opaque black, custard with green paint, and amethyst opalescent.
Black and Amethyst Opal $50-60 Others $30-40
Ref.- HC5 p. 12 (advertisement)

109. **GRAPE & FESTOON WITH SHIELD**
$1^{7}/_{8}$" dia. x $1^{7}/_{8}$" ht. or $2^{3}/_{8}$" dia. x $2^{3}/_{8}$" ht. or $3^{1}/_{8}$" dia. x $3^{1}/_{4}$" ht.
Doyle & Co. made this mug in the 1870s. It was produced in clear, blue and cobalt.
All Sizes Clear $40-50 All Sizes Color $70-90
Ref.- GCF1 p. 90, PP2 p. 47, TOY p. 141, WHPG p. 129

110. **GRAPE BUNCH**
3" dia. x $3^{1}/_{2}$" ht.
This mug was made by Bryce Brothers in the 1880s and the U. S. Glass Co. after 1891. It was produced in clear, amber, blue, apple green, canary and amethyst. This mug is the second largest in a graduated 4 piece set. The other mugs are Chick & Pugs, Feeding Deer & Dog and Robin in Tree. Strawberry & Pear has the same shape and handle.
Clear $25-35 Colors $35-45
Ref.- HC5 p. 81 (advertisement)

111. **STRAWBERRY & PEAR**
3" dia. x $3^{3}/_{8}$" ht.
Bryce Brothers probably was the maker of this mug in the 1880s because of the shape and the handle style. It also may have been manufactured by the U. S. Glass Co after 1891. It was made in clear, amber, blue and canary. There is a graduated 4 mug set which shares the shape and handle design. Similar mugs are Chick & Pugs, Feeding Deer & Dog, Grape Bunch and Robin in Tree. There is an 8 pointed star on the bottom of this mug. A reproduction was made in the 1940s with a 24 pointed star.
Clear $30-40 Color $45-55
Ref.- None

112. **INTERTWINED GRAPE**
$2^{1}/_{4}$" dia. x $3^{1}/_{8}$" ht.
This flint mug was probably made in England or Europe in the 1880s. It was produced in clear with enameled green leaves, purple grapes and a gold band at the top.
Clear with Enamel $60-70
Ref.- None

sm, 113

lg. 113

114

115

116

117

113. **RINGED GRAPE**
2 1/2" dia. x 3" ht. or 2 3/4" dia. x 3 1/4" ht.
These flint mugs were probably manufactured in England or Europe in the 1880s. They are known in blue and opaque blue. These are likely companion mugs to the Ringed Flowering Raspberry mugs.
Both Sizes and Colors $60-75
Ref.- None

114. **STIPPLED FUSHIA**
2 3/4" dia. x 4" ht.
This flint mug was probably made in England or Europe in the 1880s. It is only known in green. The flower shown on this mug is identical to the flower on the Fuchsia pattern.
Clear $50-65
Ref.- None

115. **BOHEMIAN (FLORODORA)**
2 3/8" dia. x 3 1/2" ht.
The U. S. Glass Co. manufactured this scarce pattern about 1899. The mug is rare. It was made in clear, green, clear with rose stain and gold, and frosted with rose and yellow stain. Over 20 different pieces were made in this pattern.
Clear $60-75
Stained and Green $125-150
Ref.- WHPG p. 47

116. **ORANGE TREE**
3 1/2" dia. x 3 1/2" ht. or another size
The Fenton Art Glass Co. manufactured this pattern after 1910. The pattern was produced in chocolate, light green and various carnival colors: amber, marigold, amethyst, blue, and green. It is rare in white, red, lime opalescent, ice green, black and aqua. The irridecence isn't as vibrant in the reissued mug.
Marigold, Amethyst,
Blue and Green $40-60
Amber $150-175
Other Carnival Colors $400+
Ref.- CARN p. 144,
HCG1 p. 6 and 9 (advertisement)

117. **DAHLIA**
2 5/8" dia. x 2 3/4" ht. or
3 1/8" dia. x 3 1/4" ht.
Portland Glass Co., Canton Glass Co., Burlington Glass Works and Diamond Flint Glass Co. all manufactured this pattern between 1865 and 1890. All items in the pattern were made in clear, amber, blue, canary and apple green. Over 25 different pieces were made in this pattern.
Both Sizes Clear $30-40
Both Sizes Color $50-60
Ref.- JLPG p. 148, LEE p. 403,
MET1 p. 65, MMPG p. 268,
WHPG p. 84

118. **GRAPEVINE (VINE)**
1 7/8" dia. x 1 7/8" ht. or 2" dia. x 2 3/8" ht. or 2 1/2" dia. x 2 5/8" ht. or 3" dia. x 3" ht.
King, Son & Co. made this mug in the 1870s. It was produced in clear, amber and cobalt.
All Sizes in Clear $20-35 All Sizes in Color $35-55
Ref.- CORN p. 166, GCF1 p. 82, PITT p. 301 (advertisement, 3 sizes shown)

119. **OPEN MOUTH**
2 1/8" dia. x 3 1/8" ht.
This flint mug was probably manufactured in England or Europe in the 1880s. It has three circles that are connected opposite the handle (which probably had a label). Grapes are in the field around the "mouth". It is known in clear only..
Clear $25-30
Ref.- None

120. **GRAPEVINE VARIANT**
2 1/2" dia. x 2 3/8" ht.
This clear mug is similar Grapevine, with the exception of a different handle and 9 bunches of grapes instead of 6.
Clear $25-30
Ref.- None

121. **WINDING VINES**
1 1/2" dia. x 2" ht. or 1 3/4" dia. x 2" ht.
This mug was probably manufactured in the 1890s. It is known only in clear.
Both Sizes Clear $25-30
Ref.- GCF1 p. 82, PP2 p. 99

122. **FUSHIA**
1 7/8" dia. x 2 1/8" ht.
The Boston & Sandwich Glass Co. made this pattern during the 1870s. There is a 4 piece table set and a goblet, in addition to the mug. It was only produced in clear.
Clear $35-45
Ref.- LEEV p. 90 (mug not listed)

123. **GRAPE**
This mug is very simlar to Grapevine, except the handle is squared. Only known in clear.
Clear $20-25
Ref.- None

124. **LEAF & GRAPE**
2" dia. x 1 3/4" ht. (saucer not shown)
This cup and saucer was probably produced after 1900. It is known only in clear.
Clear $25-30 50% less without saucer
Ref.- TOY p. 133

125. **GRAPEVINE WITH OVALS**
1 7/8" dia. x 1 7/8" ht.
McKee & Brothers made this mug in the 1870s. It was produced in clear, amber, blue, opaque white and possibly other colors.
Clear $25-30 Colors $35-45
Ref.- GR2, MK p. 88 (advertisement, but not mug), TOY p. 158

126. **CABBAGE ROSE**
This tumbler with applied handled was manufactured by the Central Glass Co. The pattern was designed and patented by John Oesterling on July 26, 1870. It was made only in clear. Over 60 different items were made in the pattern.
Clear $50-60
Ref.- JLPG p. 99, PG&B p. 113 (advertisement), WEPG p. 243

127. **BLEEDING HEART**
2 3/8"dia. x 3 1/4" ht.
The Westmoreland Specialty Co. was the maker of this mug about 1888. It was made in clear and opalescent—both painted with dull gold. It was sold as a condiment container with a tin cover. Bleeding Heart was made in 65 different pieces by King, Sons & Co., Boston & Sandwich Glass Co., The Burlington Glass Works, and the U. S. Glass Co. between 1875 and 1900.
Clear $40-50 Opalescent $75-95 add 25% for good paint or tin cover
Ref.- JLPG p. 72, KM8 p. 180 (advertisement), LEE p. 400, MET1 p. 59, MMPG p. 266, PITT p. 418, TOY p. 141, WHPG p. 44

128. **RINGED GRAPEVINE**
2 3/8" dia. x 3 5/8" ht.
This flint mug was probably manufactured in England or Europe in the 1880s. It is known only in clear.
Clear $45-55
Ref.- None

129. **CUT WILD ROSE**
2 7/8" dia. x 3 5/8" ht.
The Cambridge Glass Co. made this mug about 1906. It was produced in clear, rose stain came later.
Clear $10-15
Ref.- KM8 p. 202 (advertisement)

118
119
120
121
122
123
124
125
126
127
128
129

130

131

137

130. **BEADS IN RELIEF**

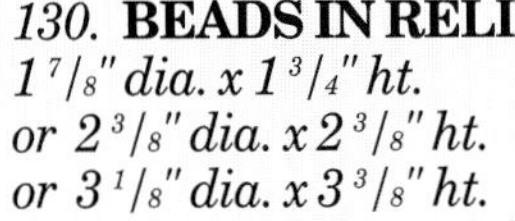

$1^{7}/_{8}$" dia. x $1^{3}/_{4}$" ht.
or $2^{3}/_{8}$" dia. x $2^{3}/_{8}$" ht.
or $3^{1}/_{8}$" dia. x $3^{3}/_{8}$" ht.

This mug was manufactured about 1880. It has ornate beads and scrolls with grapes. The two larger sizes have blank medallions on the front, possibly for a label. They may have been "packer's ware" with mustard or ointment inside. Some mugs have a star on the bottom, while others do not. There are several handle variations. These were produced in clear, opaque blue, Blue opalescent, opalescent and cobalt.

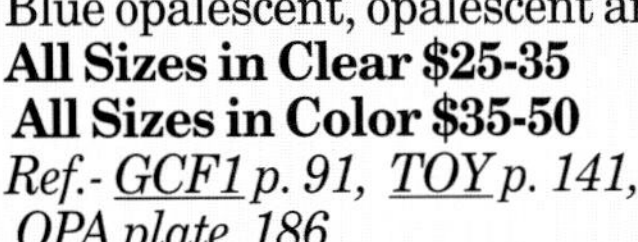

All Sizes in Clear $25-35
All Sizes in Color $35-50
Ref.- GCF1 p. 91, TOY p. 141, OPA plate 186

131. **HOLLY (NATIONAL'S NO. 450)**
$2^{5}/_{8}$" dia. x $4^{3}/_{4}$" ht.

The National Glass Co. (at the Indiana Tumbler & Goblet Works) manufactured this pattern from January to June, 1903, when production was stopped because the factory burned. The unique color was originally called Golden Agate, but collectors today call it Holly Amber. The mug is known in clear and Golden Agate. It was reproduced in various colors by the St. Clair Glass Co. of Elwood, Indiana.

Clear $60-70
Golden Agate. $400-500
Ref.- GRE fig.231, MMPG p. 408, WEPG p. 241, WHPG p. 144

138

139

140

141

142

143

132

132

133

134

135

144

145

146

132. **ROSE IN SNOW**
3 1/4" dia. x 3 3/4" ht. (handled water tumbler) or 3" dia. x 3 1/2" ht. (In Fond Rem. front) or 3" dia. x 3 3/8" ht. (In Fond Rem. side)
Bryce Brothers manufactured the pattern in the 1880s. After 1891, it was made by the U. S. Glass Co. About 1898, it was manufactured by the Ohio Flint Glass Co. It was made in clear, amber, blue, pink, canary and with gold. There are about 35 different items in the pattern.
Applied Handle Clear $30-40
Other Types Clear $25-35
All Sizes Amber, Pink and Canary $40-50 All Sizes Blue $90-110
Ref.- GCF2 p. 190, LEE p. 372, JLPG p. 454, MET1 p. 55, WEPG p. 243 and 329

133. **STIPPLED ROSE & LILY OF THE VALLEY / IN FOND REMEMBERENCE**
3" dia. x 3 1/2" ht.
Bryce Brothers made this mug in the 1880s, and the U. S. Glass Co. made it after 1891. It has a rose similar to Stippled Rose & Lily of the Valley, except the front medallion says "IN FOND REMEMBERENCE". It is made in clear, amber and possibly in other colors.
Clear $35-40 Color $50-65
Ref.- PG&B p. 90 (advertisement)

134. **ROSE SPRIG**
3 3/8" dia. x 3 3/4" ht.
Campbell, Jones & Co. manufactured this pattern. It was designed and patented May 25, 1886 by Henry Franz. A handled water tumbler is shown. It was made in clear, amber, blue and canary. There are over 30 different items in the pattern.
Clear $40-45 Color $50-60
Ref.- JLPG p. 454, MET1 p. 55, MMPG p. 250, WHPG p. 225

135. **VINTAGE BANDED**
3 1/4" dia. x 3 1/4" ht.
The Dugan Glass Co. and its successor, the Diamond Glass-Ware Co., probably made this mug between 1910 and 1922. It was made in marigold carnival and smoke carnival.
Marigold $30-35 Smoke $40-45
Ref.- CARN p. 210

136

136. **BRAZIL (PANELLED DAISY)**
3 1/8" dia. x 3 3/4" ht.
The pattern was made by Bryce Brothers in the 188s and by the U. S. Glass Co. after 1891. It was produced in clear and is rare in amber stain. Over 20 different pieces were made in this pattern.
Clear $35-45 Amber $70-90
Ref.- HC5 p. 74 (advertisement), JLPG p. 395, MET1 p. 63

137. **DANDELION**
3 1/2" dia. x 3 5/8" ht.
The H. Northwood Co. of Wheeling, West Virginia, first produced this mug about 1911. The mug was made in the carnival colors: marigold, amethyst, green, blue, white, green opalescent, blue opalescent, aqua opalescent, ice blue and ice green. See Dandelion - Knight's Templar in the Historic section.
Marigold, Amethyst and Blue $400-475 Green and Aqua Opal. $500-575 Green Opal. and Blue Opal. $550-650 Ice Blue and Ice Green $650-850
Ref.- CARN p. 58

138. **IVY IN SNOW (PHOENIX'S FOREST WARE)**
3" dia. x 3" ht.
The Co-Operative Flint Glass Co. made this pattern starting in 1898. In 1937, the Phoenix Glass Co. took molds for 5 patterns from Co-Operative to help settle a debt. Ivy in Snow was one of those patterns. It was produced in clear, amber stain, ruby stain, blue and opaque white. White was only made in Phoenix. Over 25 different pieces were made in this pattern.
Clear and Opaque White $30-35 Blue and Stained $75-100
Ref.- JLPG p. 296, KM3 p. 146 (advertisement)

139. **RIBBED FORGET-ME-NOT (PERT)**
2 1/2" dia. x 3 1/8" ht.
Bryce Brothers made this pattern in the 1880s. After 1891, it was made by the U. S. Glass Co. A U. S. Glass Co. catalogue shows an advertisement for the mug as a mustard with a cover. There is a 4 piece table set. The pattern was produced in clear, amber, blue, amethyst and canary.
Clear $30-40 Colors $50-65 with cover 50% more
Ref.- GCF1 p. 92, HC5 p. 84 (advertisement), PG&B p. 86 (advertisement), MET1 p. 57, TOY p. 155, WHPG p. 219

140. **RINGED FLOWERING RASPBERRY, LARGE**
2 7/8" dia. x 3 1/2" ht.
This flint mug was probably manufactured in England or Europe in the 1880s. It is known in opaque blue. The flowers and leaves are smaller on this larger mug. This mug is most likely a companion mug to Small Ringed Flowering Raspberry and the Ringed Grape mugs.
Color $60-75
Ref.- None

141. **RINGED FLOWERING RASPBERRY, SMALL**
2 3/8" dia. x 2 3/4" ht.
This mug was probably manufactured in England or Europe in the 1880s. It is known in blue . The flowers and leaves are larger on this smaller mug. This mug is probably a companion mug to Large Ringed Flowering Raspberry and the Ringed Grape mugs.
Colors $60-75
Ref.- None

142. **ROSE PANELS**
3 1/8" dia. x 3 3/8" ht.
This mug was probably made in the early 1900s. It is known in opaque white, with gaudy red roses and showy green foliage. The hue and intensity of the applied color indicate this mug was made later. Because of the similarity in design, this mug was probably made by the same manufacturer as Cupid in Arch.
Opaque White $30-40 Good Paint $35-45
Ref.- None

143. **STUMP & VINE**
2 3/4" dia. x 2 7/8" ht.
The H. Northwood Glass Co. made this mug in the early 1900s. The vine is on the back of the stump. It was produced in blue, green, blue opalescent, green opalescent, opalescent and possibly other colors.
Color $30-35 Opal. Color $45-55
Ref.- GCF1 p. 84, HC2 p. 72

144. **WHEAT & BARLEY (DUQUESNE)**
3 1/4" dia. x 3 3/4" ht.
Bryce Brothers was the maker of this pattern in the 1880s. The U. S. Glass Co. took over production after 1891. It was made in clear, amber, blue and canary. Over 35 different pieces were made in this pattern in all colors.
Clear $25-30 Color $40-50
Ref.- JLPG p. 554, LEE p. 515, MET1 p. 85, MMPG p. 412

145. **WEE BRANCHES**
mug: 2" dia. x 2" ht. or cup and saucer: 1 7/8" dia. x 1 3/4" ht.
This mug was manufactured by the U. S. Glass Co. in the 1890s. It is part of a toy table set. It was produced in clear, blue, opaque white and opaque blue.
Mug Clear $30-35 Mug Color $40-55 Cup and Saucer Clear $45-60 50% less without saucer
Ref.- GCF1 p. 128, TOY p. 139

146. **WILLOW OAK (WREATH)**
3 1/4" dia. x 3 7/8" ht.
Bryce Brothers manufactured this pattern in the 1880s. After 1891, production was taken over by the U. S. Glass Co. It was produced in clear, amber, blue and canary. Over 25 different pieces were made in this pattern in all colors.
Clear $30-35 Color $40-55
Ref.- HC5 p. 83 (advertisement), JLPG p. 557, LEE p. 525, MMPG p. 268

132

150

152

153

147. **STIPPLED CHERRY**
p. 147 for pattern picture
The Lancaster Glass Co. was the maker of this pattern in the 1880s. It is known only in clear.
Clear $30-35
Ref.- LEE p. 476, MET1 p. 91, MMPG p. 294

148. **INVERTED STRAWBERRY**
p. 147 for pattern picture
The Cambridge Glass Co. manufactured this pattern about 1905. The mug is a tumbler with an applied handle. It is marked "Near Cut" in the bottom. The pattern was produced in clear, ruby stain and possibly other colors. Over 35 different pieces were made in this pattern. The pattern has been reproduced, but not the mug.
Clear $30-40 Color $45-60
Ref.- JLPG p. 293

149. **GOOD LUCK VARIANT**
not shown
Revi shows the patent drawing assigned to A. J. Beatty & Sons. However, I've never seen the mug so it's possible that it was never manufactured.
Ref.- PG&B p. 55 (patent drawing)

150. **RINGED HOLLY**
3" dia. x 4 1/2" ht.
This mug was probably manufactured in England in the 1880s. It has 3 holly branches on a ringed background with a twig handle. It is known in clear and purple slag.
Clear $65-75 Slag $125-150
Ref.- None

151. **GRAPE & FESTOON WITH STIPPLED LEAF**
p. 147 for pattern picture
3 1/8" dia. x 2 5/8" ht.
This pattern was manufactured by the Boston & Sandwich Glass Co. and by Doyle & Co. in the 1880s. After 1891, it was manufactured by the U.S. Glass Co. It was made only in clear. Over 25 different pieces were made in this pattern.
Clear $40-50
Ref.- LEE p. 214

152. **RIBBED LEAVES**
2 1/4" dia. x 3 3/8" ht.
It is possible that this mug was made by the Federal Glass Co., however, it is just as likely that it was made by another manufacturer at the turn of the century. It was made only in clear.
Clear $25-30
Ref.- None

154

155

156

157

153. **RIBBED LEAVES VARIANT**
2 1/2" dia. x 2 5/8" ht.
This mug was manufactured by the Federal Glass Co. It is shown in a 1914 Federal Glass Company's Packer's Catalogue. It was made only in clear.
Clear $25-30
Ref.- GCF1 p. 94, HGC4 p. 22 (advertisement), HGC5 p. 40 (advertisement), MET2 p. 207, TOY p. 143

154. **STIPPLED FORGET-ME-NOT**
mug: 1 3/4" dia. x 2 3/8" ht. or 2 5/8" dia. x 3 3/8" ht. or cup and saucer: 2 1/2" dia. x 2 3/4" ht.
The Findlay Flint Glass Co. was the maker of this pattern around 1889. It was made in clear, amber, blue, opaque white and rare in opalescent colors. Over 45 different items were made in this pattern. The children's 4 piece table set is rare.
Both Sizes Clear $30-35 Both Sizes Amber, Blue and Opaque White $40-55 Both Sizes Opal. Colors $60-80 add 25% for cup and saucer
Ref.- A&C2 p.184, FINP p. 82, JLPG p. 496, LEE p. 383, MET1 p. 57, TOY p. 140

155. **STIPPLED ROSE & LILY OF THE VALLEY**
3" dia. x 3 1/2" ht.
Bryce Brothers made this mug in the 1880s. The U. S. Glass Co. made it after 1891. It has a rose similar to Rose in Snow on one side and lily of the valley on the other with a stippled background. The front medallion contains an anchor flanked with acanthus leaves. It is known only in clear.
Clear $40-50
Ref.- PG&B p. 90 (advertisement)

156. **GOOSEBERRY**
3 1/8" dia. x 3 3/4" ht.
Shards of this pattern have been found at the Boston & Sandwich Glass Co. and the Burlington Glass Work. It was made in clear and opaque white. Over 20 different pieces were made in this pattern.
Clear $35-40 Opaque White $45-55
Ref.- JLPG p. 248, LEE p. 615, MET1 p. 89, TOY p. 140

158

159

160

161

157. **PANELLED THISTLE (DELTA)**
cup: 3" dia. x 2 7/8" ht. or mug
The J. B. Higbee Glass Co. was the maker of this pattern about 1910. The item shown is probably a custard, but a mug is also known. It may have,been made by the Jefferson Glass Co. and the Dominion Glass Co. about 1918 or later. It was made in clear and rare in ruby stain. The later companies may have been the maker of the pieces in scarce color. The pattern was reproduced using a bee formed by lines with antenae and a stinger.
Clear Cup $15-20 Clear Mug $25-30
Ref.- JLPG p. 399

158. **STRAWBERRY, FALCON (JENKINS NO. 215)**
2 1/2" dia. x 3 1/4" ht.
The D. C. Jenkins Glass Co. manufactured this pattern about 1915. It was only produced in clear. The pattern contains a 4 piece table set, a goblet, a bowl, a pitcher, a syrup and a toothpick as well as the mug.
Clear $25-30
Ref.- JJ p. 24, WHPG p. 252

159. **STIPPLED FLOWER BASKET**
2 3/8" dia. x 2 7/8" ht.
This flint mug was probably made England or Europe in the 1880s. It is known only in clear.
Clear $40-50
Ref.- None

160. **PANELLED SUNFLOWER**
2 1/2" dia. x 3 3/8" ht.
The D. C. Jenkins Glass Co. made this mug about 1920. It was only produced in clear.
Clear $25-30
Ref.- JJ p. 26, WHPG p. 196

161. **SUNFLOWER & VINES**
2 1/2" dia. x 4" ht.
This flint mug was probably manufactured in England or Europe in the 1880s. It is known only in clear.
Clear $25-30
Ref.- None

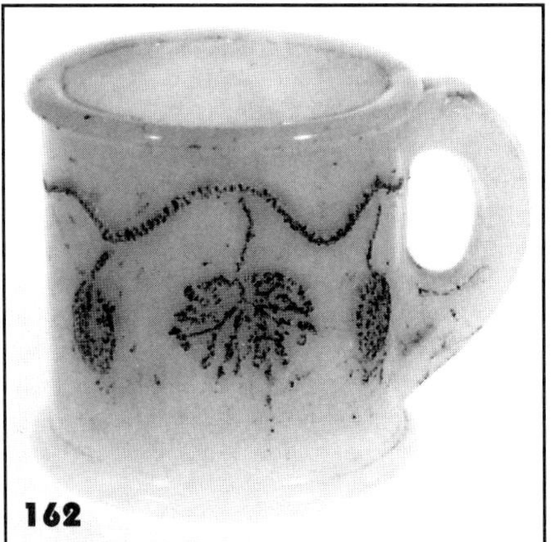
162

163

164

165

166

162. **LOGANBERRY**
1 7/8" dia. x 1 7/8" ht.
This mug was probably manufactured in the 1880s. It is known only in opaque white.
Opaque White $25-30
Ref.- HOB1, TOY p. 157

163. **LEAF, ATTERBURY'S (MELON)**
3" dia. x 3 1/2" ht.
This pattern with limited table service was manufactured by Atterbury & Co. The mug has a patent date of Apr. 23, 1878 on the bottom. It was made in clear, amber, opaque white, gray/green and possibly other colors.
Clear $50-60 Color $75-90
Ref.- GCD1, GCD2, MG p. 127 (advertisement), PITT p. 399 (advertisement, but no mug - mug gives the same patent date)

164. **OAK LEAF WREATH**
The Central Glass Co. was the maker of this mug in the 1880s. The mug is a tumbler with an applied handle. After 1891, it was made by the U. S. Glass Co. It was produced in clear and colors.
Clear $30-35
Ref.- HOB1, PG&B p. 113 (advertisement), TOY p. 157

165. **STRAWBERRY & CURRANT (3 FRUITS & OTHERS)**
3 1/2" dia. x 3 7/8" ht.
Dalzell, Gilmore & Leighton was the maker of this pattern in the 1880s. The mug is a tumbler with an applied handle. Every items has different fruits. This has confused many authors over the years, therefore, every item has has a different name. It was made only in clear.
Clear $45-55
Ref.- JLPG p. 501

166. **THISTLE**
3 3/8" dia. x 3 7/8" ht.
Known only in opaque white. this mug was produced in England in the 1880s. It has an English rose, a Scottish thistle and an Irish shamrock in high relief. It has a twig handle and twig bands at the top and bottom.
Opaque White $65-85
Ref.- None

167. **MAINE (STIPPLED PANELLED FLOWER, U. S. GLASS' NO. 15066)**
p. 147 for pattern picture
The U. S. Glass Co. was the maker of this pattern about 1899. It was made in clear, green and with stain (green, pink and white). It is a medium sized table service.
Clear $30-40
Green & Stain $80-100
Ref.- JLPG p. 347, LEE p. 423, MET1 p. 67, MMPG p. 288

168. **PANELLED GRAPE**
not shown
Mug is shown in a 1914 Federal Federal Glass Company's Packer's Catalogue. This glass was used to distribute condiments. It was made in clear.
Clear $20-25
Ref.- HGC5 p. 39 (advertisement)

LACY

169. **BRASS NAILHEAD (OPALESCENT LACE)**
$1^1/_4$" dia. x $1^3/_4$" ht.
This opalescent flint cup and saucer was produced about 1840. The saucer is a lacy cup plate.
Clear $100-125
without saucer 50% less
Ref.- MET2 p. 205, TOY p. 133

169

170. **DAISY & FLEUR-DE-LIS**
$4^3/_8$" dia. x $3^1/_4$" ht.
This large flint mug was probably made about 1835. It may have been manufactured at Baccarat in France. Its intended use remains unknown, but it was not made to have a cover. The mug is known only in clear.
Clear $150-175
Ref.- None

171. **GOTHIC ARCH & STAR**
$2^3/_8$" dia. x 3" ht.
The country of origin is uncertain for this mug, however, it was probably made about 1840. It is known only in clear. A blue 7" dia. plate is also known.
Clear $100-125
Ref.- None

172. **LACY HEART**
2" dia. x 2" ht.
The Boston & Sandwich Glass Co. made this flint mug about 1835. It was only produced in clear.
Clear $400-450
Ref.- CORN p. 80, SAN1 p. 107, SAN3 p. 216

173. **LACY FLOWER**
1 1/8" dia. x 1" ht. not shown
The Boston & Sandwich Glass Co. was the maker of this flint cup and saucer about 1835. It was made in clear, amber, red and amethyst. Colors are rare.
Clear $150-175 Amber $375-450
Red $500-600 Amethyst $550-650
50% less without saucer
Ref.- CORN p. 155, SAN3 p. 221, TOY p. 32

174. **LACY VINE**
2 1/4" dia. x 1 3/4" ht.
This mug was likely made about 1835 in France. It probably had a saucer. It is known only in clear.
Clear $70-90
Ref.- CORN p. 156 (not shown, but same handle and bowl shape)

175. **LEAF BAND & SWAG**
$2^3/_4$" dia. x 2" ht.
This flint mug was probably made about 1835. It may have been manufactured at Baccarat in France. The mug is known only in clear.
Clear $90-110
Ref.- None

170

171

172

174

175

176

177

178

179

176. **PEACOCK EYE**
$2^{3}/_{4}$" dia. x 2" ht.
This flint mug with pressed handle was made for a cover with a slot; therefore, it is a mustard. The Boston & Sandwich Glass Co. made it about 1840. The underplate that is sometimes seen with this piece does not belong, for they do not fit together properly. It was produced in clear, opalescent, cobalt and amethyst. Colors are rare.
Clear $350-425 Color $900-1100
60% less without cover
Ref.- CORN p. 85, SAN1 p. 126, SAN3 p. 197

177. **STAR & GREEK KEY**
$4^{7}/_{8}$" dia. x $3^{1}/_{2}$" ht.
This large flint mug was probably made about 1835, perhaps at Baccarat in France. The use for which it was made is unknown. It was not made to have a cover. The mug is known only in clear.
Clear $150-175
Ref.- None

178. **LACY PANELLED FLOWER**
2" dia. x $1^{1}/_{2}$" ht.
This small flint cup and saucer were probably made in England or France about 1835. They are only known in clear.
Clear $125-150
50% less without saucer
Ref.- None

179. **PANELLED FLOWER & FERN**
2" dia. x $1^{3}/_{4}$" ht.
This small flint mug was likely made about 1835. There was probably a saucer also. It is known only in clear.
Clear $70-90
Ref.- None

EARLY FLINT

180. **ASHBURTON**
2 5/8" dia. x 2 3/4" ht. or
2 3/4" dia. x 3 3/8" ht. or
large covered toddy or 4 stein sizes
Boston & Sandwich Glass Co., Bakewell, Pears & Co., New England Glass Co., Curling, Robertson & Co., C. Ihmsen & Co. and McKee & Brothers manufactured this pattern. The mugs are flint tumblers with applied handle. The pattern was probably made over a long period of time, 1850 through 1870 in flint, and about 1900 in non-flint. The mug is known only in clear. Rare colors in the rest of the pattern are: amber, blue-green, canary yellow, opalescent and opaque white. There are over 65 different pieces in the pattern.
All Mugs and Steins Clear $70-100
Covered Toddy $200-250
50% less without cover
Ref.- JLPG p. 27, LEE p. 16, MK p. 78 (advertisement), PITT p. 343, PG&B p. 253 (advertisement), WHPG p. 22, WEPG p. 243

180

181. **ASHBURTON WITH SAWTOOTH**
This flint whiskey tumbler with applied handle was made by Bryce, McKee & Co. in the 1850s and comes only in clear. Also known in a goblet, a decanter, an apothacary jar and a whiskey tumbler.
Clear $65-80
Ref.- MET2 p. 19

182. **DEEP ARCH**
2 7/8" dia. x 2 7/8" ht.
This flint whiskey tumbler with applied handle was probably made about 1860. It is known only in clear.
Clear $65-80
Ref.- None

183. **HINOTO**
2 7/8" dia. x 3 5/8" ht.
The Boston & Sandwich Glass Co. made this pattern in the late 1850s. The flint mug is a whiskey tumbler with an applied handle. It was made in clear and possibly a rare canary.
Clear $100-125
Ref.- SAN1 p. 157 (mug not shown)

184. **LOOP VARIANT**
2 5/8" dia. x 3" ht.
The maker of this flint whiskey tumbler with applied handle could have been any one of many. It was probably made in the 1860s. Only known in clear.
Clear $60-75
Ref.- None

185. **HORN OF PLENTY**
2 3/4" dia. x 3" ht.
The Boston & Sandwich Glass Co., McKee & Brothers and perhaps others made this pattern between 1850 and 1870. There is reason to believe that the maker of the pattern Festoon also made this pattern and that it was neither of these companies. I have a cakestand with a non-flint Festoon top and

181

182

183

184

185

186

187

188

189

190

191

a flint Horn of Plenty base. This base was made in the same mold as the base on the 9 ½" Horn of Plenty compote. A flint applied handle whiskey tumbler is shown. The mug is known only in clear. The pattern has about 45 different items and many of them are rare. The pattern was made in clear, amber, canary, black amber, electric blue, cobalt, amethyst, opalescent and clear with colored glass applied to the rim. The pattern is very rare in color.
Clear $350-400
Ref.- AG p. 405, CORN p. 259, JLPG p. 284, LEE p. 152, MMPG p. 76, WEPG p. 243

186. **DIAMOND POINT**
2 3/4" dia. x 3" ht.
A flint handled whiskey tumbler is shown. This pattern was made by the New England Glass Co. and the Boston & Sandwich Glass Co. between 1850 and 1870. The mug is known only in clear. The pattern is rare in blue, amethyst, canary, opaque white, clambroth, canary clambroth and green clambroth. The table service has over 75 different items.
Clear $125-150
Ref.- JLPG p. 179, LEE p. 137, MET1 p. 35

187. **DIAMOND THUMBPRINT (DIAMOND & CONCAVE)**
2 5/8" dia. x 3" ht.
The Boston & Sandwich Glass Co. and the Union Glass Co. were the makers of this flint pattern about 1850. A flint handled whiskey tumbler is shown. The pattern is known in clear and canary, but the mug is known only in clear. The pattern has over 75 different pieces with many compote sizes and shapes. The rarest items are a wine jug with places to hang glasses and a double burner whale oil lamp that feeds from a font, in the middle, to both burners. (one piece, all glass).
Clear $325-375
Ref.- AG p. 404, JLPG p. 184

188. **FLUTE**
many sizes.
Bakewell, Pears & Co., C. Ihmsen & Co., Adams & Co. and McKee & Brothers all manufactured this flint pattern from 1840 to 1870. The pattern is shown in an 1856 Curling, Robertson & Co. catalogue. It made in clear, is rare in blue, except pressed handle mugs and tumblers. Other colors are rare. Pressed handles in the smaller sizes are common. There are about 45 different items in the pattern.
Pressed Handle in Clear $35-40
Pressed Handle in Blue $45-55
Pressed Handle in Other Colors $70-90 Applied Handle in Clear $50-60 All Applied Handle in Color $100-125
Ref.- JLPG p. 226, PITT p. 304 (advertisement but no mug), SAN3 p. 217, WEPG p. 243

189. **HAMILTON**
2 1/2" dia. x 2 7/8" ht.
This is a flint whiskey tumbler with an applied handle. The Boston & Sandwich Glass Co. and the Cape Cod Glass Co. were the makers of this pattern in the 1860s. The mug is known in clear. The pattern is rare in deep blue or opalescent. There are about 30 different items in the pattern.
Clear $150-175
Ref.- JLPG p. 258

190. **HAIRPIN (SANDWICH LOOP)**
2 3/4" dia. x 2 7/8" ht. or larger
The Boston & Sandwich Glass Co. made this pattern, which includes flint applied handle tumblers, about 1850. All items in the pattern as well as the

192

Way - 196

196

195

197

198

mug were made in clear and opalescent. There are about 20 different items in the pattern.
Both Sizes Clear $45-55
Both Sizes Opalescent $125-150
Ref.- JLPG p. 256, WHPG p. 132

191. **HONEYCOMB**
New York - handled whiskey:
2 3/8" dia. x 2 3/4" ht.
or Vernon - stein: 1 3/4" dia. x 3 3/8" ht.
This pattern was manufactured by more than a dozen factories between 1850 and 1900. The mug is a flint whiskey tumbler with an applied handle. The mug is known in clear and would be rare in color. Honeycomb was made in several variations including Cincinnati, New York and Vernon. It was produced in flint and non-flint. The table service for this pattern has over 120 items including all variations.
Clear Stein $60-75
Applied Handle in Clear $60-100
Ref.- AG p. 405, GCF1 p. 80, JLPG p. 281, LEE p. 195, PITT p. 309 (advertisement), TOY p. 143

192. **GOTHIC**
2 1/4" dia. x 3 3/8" ht.
This is an egg cup with an applied handle and was probably not part of standard production. The Boston & Sandwich Glass Co. and the Union Glass Co. made this flint pattern about 1860. Only produced in clear, this pattern contains about 25 different items.
Clear $100-125
Ref.- JLPG p. 249 (mug not listed)

193. **COMET**
p. 147 for pattern picture
Boston & Sandwich Glass Co. was the maker of this flint pattern in the 1850s. The mug is made from a whiskey tumbler and has an applied handle. The pattern was produced in clear and is rare in canary yellow and bright blue. The mug is known only in clear. There is a 4 piece table set, a goblet, a compote, a mug, a water tumbler and a whiskey tumbler.
Clear $300-350
Ref.- JLPG p. 128

194. **HAMILTON WITH LEAF**
p. 169 for pattern picture
This is a flint applied handle whiskey tumbler. The Cape Cod Glass Co. manufactured this pattern in the 1860s. The mug is known in clear and frosted (machine ground leaf). There are about 20 different items in the pattern.
Clear $150-175 Frosted $200-250
Ref.- JLPG p. 259 (mug picture shown), LEE p. 177, MET2 p. 49

195. **B.V.**
2 7/8" dia. x 3" ht. and Stein
McKee & Brothers show the stein in their 1864 catalogue. The flint mug is a whiskey tumbler with an applied handle.
Both Clear $60-75
Ref.- MKVG p. 40 (advertisement), PITT p. 343

196. **COLONIAL**
1 5/8" dia. x 1 3/4" ht. or
2 5/8" dia. x 2 3/4" ht. or
Way Colonial- 3 1/8" dia. x 3 1/2" ht.
Boston & Sandwich Glass Co. was the maker of this flint pattern in the 1850s and 60s. The pattern is shown in an 1856 Curling, Robertson & Co. advertisement. The mug is made from a whiskey tumbler and has an applied handle. The Way Colonial variation is also shown. The pattern was produced in clear and is rare in opalescent.
All Sizes Clear $80-100
Ref.- WEPG p. 243

199

200

201

202

203

204

197. **PITT DIAMOND (PITT HONEYCOMB)**
3 3/8" dia. x 4" ht.
This pattern is shown in a catalog by Bakewell, Pears & Co. from about 1876. A flint applied handle water tumbler is shown. The pattern has over 20 different pieces. It is known only in clear.
Clear $100-125
Ref.- BAKE p.6 (advertisement, mug not shown), MET1 p. 43

198. **PILLAR**
3 1/4" dia. x 3 7/8" ht.
This pattern is shown in a catalog by Bakewell, Pears & Co. from about 1876. A flint handled water tumbler is shown. It is known only in clear.
Clear $100-125
Ref.- BAKE p.5 (advertisement, mug not shown), MET1 p. 24

199. **OHIO (PILLAR VARIANT)**
smaller or 3" dia. x 4 1/4" ht.
This applied handle stein is shown in a Jan. 1, 1860 H. L. Ringwald's 2nd Annual Circular. The manufacturer was probably located in Pittsburgh, Pa. It is known only in clear.
Both Sizes Clear $60-75
Ref.- PITT p. 309 (advertisement)

200. **HUBER (CRYSTAL)**
handled whiskey: 2 5/8" dia. x 3" ht. or handled egg cup: 2 3/4" dia. x 3 7/8" ht. or stein: 2 1/2" dia. x 3 1/2" ht.
Many manufacturers made this pattern. It was produced in flint in the 1860s. McKee & Brothers show the Crystal mug in its 1859-60 catalogue, while both Crystal and Huber are shown in its 1868 and 1871 catalogues. It was made in clear and etched.
Mug and Stein Clear $45-55
Handled Egg Cup Clear $55-60
Ref.- MKVG p. 25 and 173 (advertisement, mug and egg cup)
BAKE p.8 (advertisement, stein)

201. **RINGED FRAMED OVALS**
3 1/8" dia. x 3 7/8" ht.
This flint applied handle tumbler was probably manufactured by the New England Glass Co. about 1860. A goblet and a tumbler are also known. They were produced in clear, green and canary. Colors are rare.
Clear $125-150
Ref.- MET2 p. 10, WHPG p. 222 (mug not listed)

205

202. **SHORT LOOPS**
1 1/2" dia. x 1 5/8" ht.
This flint mug is a pressed handle whiskey taster from the 1860s and is a Flute variant. It was made in clear and blue. Barlow and Kaiser in SAN3 p. 217 call these small flint mugs "lemonades."
Clear $35-40
Blue $75-90
Ref.- MET2 p. 205

200

206

207

208

209

210

203. **PERSIAN SPEAR**
3 1/8" dia. x 4" ht.
This clear flint mug was manufactured in England in the 1870s. In the reference, it is captioned, "Tankard showing pillar design". A compote, a decanter and a goblet were also made.
Clear $50-60
Ref.- ENGP p. 27

204. **SMALL FLOWERED TULIPS**
1 3/4" dia. x 1 7/8" ht.
This flint mug with pressed handle was manufactured about 1860. It is known in clear and cobalt. Barlow and Kaiser in SAN3 p. 217 call these small flint mugs "lemonades."
Clear $40-50 Cobalt $90-110
Ref.- GCF1 p. 87, MET2 p. 205

205. **RIBBED IVY**
2 3/8" dia. x 2 3/4" ht. or another
The Boston & Sandwich Glass Co. was the maker of this pattern about 1850. A flint whiskey tumbler with an applied handled is shown. There is also a handled water tumbler. This clear pattern was made in over 35 different items.
Clear $150-175
Ref.- JLPG p. 441, LEE p. 109

206. **EGG & DART**
3 1/4" dia. x 4" ht.
The maker of this flint mug is unknown, but it appears to be English or European and is most likely from the 1860s. The mug has a pressed handle and is clear.
Clear $50-60
Ref.- None

207. **YOKED LOOP**
2 7/8" dia. x 3 1/4" ht.
This flint pattern was manufactured in the 1860s. The mug is a whiskey tumbler with an applied handle. There is a goblet, a covered sugar and a whiskey tumbler known in the pattern. It is known only in clear.
Clear $65-80
Ref.- MET1 p. 26 (mug not listed)

208. **PLAIN OVAL**
1 1/2" dia. x 1 3/8" ht.
This flint toy mug was probably made about 1850. There was probably a saucer to go with the mug. It is known only in clear.
Clear $40-50
Ref.- GCF1 p. 51

209. **HONEYCOMB WITH OVALS**
2 3/8" dia. x 3 3/8" ht.
This flint stein was probably made about 1870. It is known only in clear.
Clear $60-75
Ref.- MET1 p. 28 (mug not listed)

210. **BULLSEYE (LAWRENCE)**
smaller or 2 7/8" dia. x 3 3/8" ht. This flint pattern was made at Boston & Sandwich Glass Co. and the New England Glass Co. Items of interest include a whiskey tumbler and a water tumbler with applied handles. The pattern was made from about 1850 to 1860. The mugs are known only in clear. Rare colors that other items in the pattern were made in are: opalescent and opaque white. The pattern has about 40 different pieces.
Both Sizes Clear $100-125
Ref.- JLPG p. 88, LEE p. 155, MET1 p. 13

211

212

213

214

215

216

211. **WORCESTER**
3" dia. x 3 3/8" ht.
The Boston & Sandwich Glass Co. made this flint pattern from 1850 through 1870, and it is shown in an 1869 New England Glass Co. catalogue. The mug is a whiskey tumbler with an applied handle. The pattern was made in amber, blue, cobalt, canary yellow, green and amethyst.
Clear $100-125
Ref.-SAN1 p. 148 (mug not shown)

212. **LOOP & PETALS**
2 3/4" dia. x 4" ht.
This flint handled stein was produced about 1860 and is known only in clear. There is a rare amber stained goblet.
Clear $100-125
Ref.- MET1 p. 11 (mug not listed)

213. **OVAL & CIRCLE**
2 3/8" dia. x 3 3/8" ht. or 2 7/8" dia. x 4" ht. or Variation- 2 3/8" dia. x 3 3/4" ht.
It was about 1865 that this flint big handled stein was manufactured by Atterbury & Co. The patent drawing shows a picture of Lincoln on the bottom. There are 2 mold variations. It was made only in clear.
All Sizes Clear $100-125
Ref.- PG&B p.34 (patent drawing)

214. **SCROLLED PANELS**
3" dia. x 3 1/2" ht. or 3 3/8" dia. x 4 1/8" ht.
These flint mugs with pressed handles were probably manufactured in Europe about 1860 in clear glass.
Both Sizes Clear $40-50
Ref.- None

215. **FRAMED STAR IN OVAL**
3 1/2" dia. x 4" ht.
This flint mug has a pressed handle. The style and design of this mug indicates it's from the 1850s. It is known only in clear.
Clear $100-125
Ref.- None

216. **LONG OVAL WITH BISECTING LINES**
2 7/8" dia. x 4 1/8" ht.
The Boston & Sandwich Glass Co. was the maker of this flint pattern in the 1850s. A tumbler, a cologne and a vase are also known in this pattern. It was made in clear, canary, green, opalescent and clambroth.
Clear $100-125
Ref.- SAN3 p. 65 (mug not listed)

217

218

219

220

221

222

217. **ARGUS**
2 7/8" dia. x 2 7/8" ht.
This flint whiskey tumbler with applied handle was made at Boston & Sandwich Glass Co. and McKee & Brothers. It was probably made over a long period of time, about 1850 through 1870. It was produced only in clear. There are over 45 different items in the pattern.
Clear $100-125
Ref.- JLPG p. 21, LEE p. 19, MMPG p. 44

218. **ELONGATED DOUBLE FLUTE (ASHBURTON)**
2 3/8" dia. x 3 3/8" ht.
This flint big handled stein was made about 1870 by Bakewell, Pears & Co. and McKee & Brothers. It was only produced in clear.
Clear $100-125
Ref.- BAKE p.3 (advertisement) MKVG p.181 (advertisement)

219. **OVAL & SHIELD**
2 3/4" dia. x 4" ht.
The flint big handled stein that is shown was made about 1865. It was only produced in clear.
Clear $100-125
Ref.- None

220. **BEADED CIRCLE**
2 5/8" dia. x 3" ht.
The Boston & Sandwich Glass Co. was the maker of this mug about 1870. It was produced in flint and has an applied handle. It was made in clear and opaque white.
Clear $70-85
Opaque White $150-175
Ref.- MET2 p. 127

221. **EXCELSIOR VARIANT**
2 1/4" dia. x 3 1/8" ht.
This flint pressed handle mug was probably made in the 1870s. It's known only in clear.
Clear $40-50
Ref.- None

222. **EXCELSIOR**
3 1/8" dia. x 3 1/4" ht.
The Boston & Sandwich Glass Co., C. Ihmsen & Co. and McKee & Brothers were the manufacturers of this pattern between 1850 and 1870. A flint applied handle whiskey tumbler is shown. The mug is known only in clear. The pattern was made in clear and is rare in opalescent. The pattern has over 45 different pieces.
Clear $100-125
Ref.- AG p. 404, JLPG p. 198

223. **BAKEWELL BLOCK**
p. 147 for pattern picture
Bakewell, Pears & Co. produced this pattern about 1860. The mug is a flint whiskey tumbler with an applied handle. It is known only in clear. Over 30 different pieces were made in this pattern.
Clear $125-150
Ref.- MET1 p. 25

224. **BELLFLOWER (RIBBED LEAF)**
2 5/8" dia. x 3" ht.
This flint whiskey tumbler with applied handle was manufactured at Boston & Sandwich Glass Co. and Bryce, McKee & Co. It was made from 1850 through 1870. There are over 120 different items in the pattern. There are several variations in the pattern. There is single vine with fine rib, single vine with coarse rib, double vine with fine rib and double vine with coarse rib. The mug is known only in clear. The pattern was produced in clear, amber, cobalt, sapphire blue, opalescent, opaque white and opaque blue. It is rare in color.
Clear $250-300
Ref.- JLPG p. 62, LEE p. 97, MET1 p. 31, MMPG p. 260, WHPG p. 38

225. **BELTED WORCESTER**
p. 147 for pattern picture
This flint whiskey tumbler with applied handle was manufactured about 1860. The pattern is known only in clear.
Clear $80-100
Ref.- MET1 p. 21, WEPG p. 243

226. **BIGLER (FLUTE & SPLIT)**
p. 147 for pattern picture
Boston & Sandwich Glass Co. made this pattern as well as this flint whiskey tumbler with applied handle about 1860. The mug is known only in clear. Other items in the pattern were made in rare colors: canary yellow and amethyst. This pattern has a 4 piece table set and about 20 other items.
Clear $80-100
Ref.- JLPG p. 66, LEE p. 48, MET1 p. 21, WHPG p. 41

227. **FINE RIB**
1 5/8" dia. x 1 3/4" ht. or larger
This is a flint whiskey tumbler with an applied handle. The Boston & Sandwich Glass Co., McKee & Brothers and the New England Glass Co. made this pattern in the 1860s. The mug is known in clear, red, green and amethyst. Colors are rare. This mug was also made with cut circles and cut bellflower. There are over 80 different items in this pattern.
Pressed Handle in Clear $35-40
Applied Handle in Clear $90-110
Pressed Handle in Color $150-200
Applied Handle in Color $275-325
Cut Circles $200-250
Ref.- JLPG p. 214, LEE p. 111, MET1 p. 51, SAN3 p. 218

228. **FLUTED HEXAGON**
2 3/8" dia. x 1 7/8" ht.
This small flint cup and saucer was made about 1850 and is known only in clear.
Clear $100-125
without saucer 50% less
Ref.- GCF1 p. 51

229. **PRISM PANEL**
1 3/4" dia. x 1 5/8" ht.
The Boston & Sandwich Glass Co. manufactured this flint mug with a pressed handle in the 1860s. This mug was produced in clear, amber, blue, red, green and amethyst. Barlow and Kaiser call these small flint mugs "lemonades."
Clear $35-40 Color $125-200
Ref.- SAN3 p. 217

224

227

228

229

230

231

232

233

234

235

236

230. **PRISM**
1 3/4" dia. x 2" ht.
McKee & Brother made this pattern in the 1860s. It is known in clear and is rare in color.
Clear $40-45
Ref.- MKVG p. 58 (advertisement, but mug not shown)

231. **RINGED PANELS**
2 1/4" dia. x 2 5/8" ht. or
3 1/4" dia. x 3 5/8" ht.
These flint pressed handle mugs were probably manufactured about 1860. They were produced in clear and amethyst. This mug is very similar to Ringed Zigzag Panels and was probably made at the same factory.
Both Sizes Clear $35-60
Both Sizes Amethyst $110-145
Ref.- None

232. **TULIP**
2 5/8" dia. x 2 7/8" ht.
This flint pattern was made by Bryce, Richards & Co. in the late 1850s and by the McKee & Brothers in the 1860s. The mug is a whiskey tumbler with an applied handle. The pattern was produced in clear and is rare in opaque white. There are about 25 different pieces in the pattern.
Clear $70-90
Ref.- WHPG p. 269 MKVG p.24 (advertisement, &42 but no mug)

233. **WAFFLE & DRAPE**
3" dia. x 2 3/4" ht.
This flint pattern was probably made in France in the 1850s. A celery and a creamer have also been seen. It is known only in clear. The mug has a pressed handle.
Clear$80-100
Ref.- WEPG p. 66 (mug not listed)

234. **WAFFLE**
2 5/8" dia. x 3 1/8" ht.
The Boston & Sandwich Glass Co. was the maker of this flint pattern in the 1850s. A whiskey tumbler with an applied handle is shown. The pattern was made in clear with a few rare pieces in opaque white. There are about 35 different items in the pattern.
Clear $125-150
Ref.- JLPG p. 544, MET2 p. 19

235. **TRIANGULAR PRISM**
1 5/8" dia. x 1 3/4" ht.
This 1850s flint pattern with pressed handle is known only in clear. Barlow & Kaiser in SAN3 p. 217 call these small flint mugs "lemonades."
Clear $40-50
Ref.- SW3, WHPG p. 268

236. **RINGED ZIGZAG PANELS**
3 3/8" dia. x 3 3/4" ht.
This flint pressed handle mugs were probably manufactured about 1860. It is known only in clear. This mug is very similar to Ringed Panels and was probably made at the same factory.
Both Sizes Clear $60-75
Ref.- None

237. **WAFFLE & THUMBPRINT**
p. 147 for pattern picture
Curling, Robertson & Co. show this flint pattern in their 1856 catalogue. It is also shown in the 1869 New England Glass Co. catalogue. The mug is a whiskey tumbler with an applied handle. The pattern was produced in clear, opaque white and canary. Colors are rare. There are over 30 different items in this pattern.
Clear $150-175
Ref.- JLPG p. 544

238. **TULIP WITH SAWTOOTH**
p. 147 for pattern picture
This flint pattern was manufactured by Bryce, Richards & Co. about 1854. The mug is an applied handle whiskey tumbler and is known only in clear. The pattern was produced in clear, opaque white and opalescent. Colors are rare. About 35 different items were made in the pattern. The U. S. Glass Co. reissued some of the items in non-flint glass.
Clear $125-150
Ref.- JLPG p. 530, LEE p. 169, MET1 p. 33

239. **BULLSEYE WITH FLEUR-DE-LIS**
p. 147 for pattern picture
The Boston & Sandwich Glass Co. and the Union Glass Co. were the manufacturers of this flint pattern. This whiskey tumbler with applied handle was made about 1850 in clear. The pattern was aslo made in a rare amber. There are about 30 different pieces in this pattern.
Clear $300-350
Ref.- JLPG p. 91, MMPG p. 50

240. **NEW ENGLAND PINEAPPLE**
p. 147 for pattern picture
This is a flint whiskey tumbler with an applied handle. The Boston & Sandwich Glass Co. and the New England Glass Co. made this pattern in the 1860s. The mug is known in clear only. There are about 35 different items in the pattern and is rare in opalescent.
Clear $275-350
Ref.- JLPG p. 382, LEE p. 162, MET1 p. 13

241. **WASHINGTON**
2 sizes (beer and lemonade)
p. 147 for pattern picture
This clear flint pattern is shown in the 1869 New England Glass Co. catalogue. Over 85 different items were made in this pattern.
Both Sizes Clear $150-175
Ref.- JLPG p. 547

242. **THUMBPRINT (ARGUS)**
stein: 2 5/8" dia. x 3 3/4" ht. or 2 other sizes or mug
Bakewell, Pears & Co. was the maker of this flint pattern in the 1860s and 70s. This stein was made only in clear. About 45 different pieces were made in the pattern.
All Sizes in Clear $60-75
Ref.- BAKE p.3 (advertisement), JLPG p. 522, MET2 p. 43

243. **DOUBLE PRISM & SAWTOOTH**
2 7/8" dia. x 2 5/8" ht.
This is a pressed handle mug from about 1845. There is a lip inside the rim, indicating that it may have held a cover for a mustard. The mug is known only in clear.
Clear $50-60
Ref.- None

244. **PRISM & CRESCENT**
The Boston & Sandwich Glass Co. was the manufacturer of this pattern about 1850. A drawing of a flint whiskey tumbler with an applied handle is shown. This pattern, made in clear only, includes a champagne, a goblet, a whiskey tumbler, a water tumbler, and a lamp as well as the mug.
Clear $125-150
Ref.- LEEV p. 54, MET1 p. 19, MMPG p. 52

245. **DIAMONDS & PRISMS**
2" dia. x 2 1/4" ht.
This flint mug, known only in clear, was manufactured in the 1860s. It has a rayed base.
Clear $50-60
Ref.- None

246. **DIAMONDS & PRISMS VARIANT**
not shown
The Wear Flint Glass Co. in Sunderland, England was the maker of this 1860s mug, which is similar to the one listed above. It displays the "lion holding a star" trademark and was made in clear and cobalt.
Clear $50-60 Cobalt $80-100
Ref.- P&L plate 72

242

243

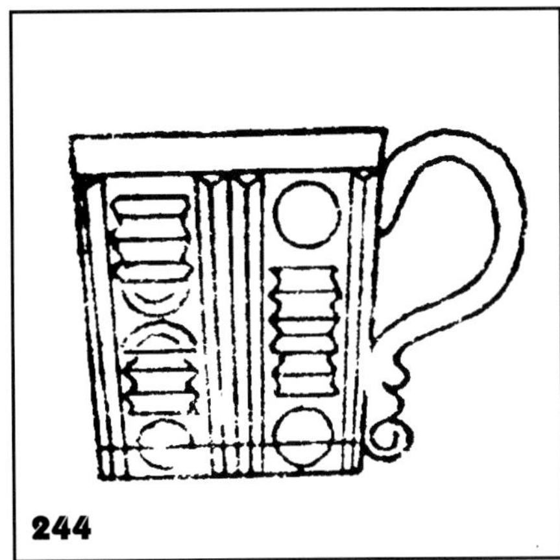
244

245

247

248

249

250

188

251

247. **ARCHES**
$2^1/_8$" dia. x $2^3/_8$" ht.
This is a flint pressed handle whiskey taster was probably made about 1860. Produced in clear and blue, this mug could be refered to as a Hairpin Variant. Barlow and Kaiser in SAN3 p. 217 call these small flint mugs "lemonades."
Clear $35-40 Blue $40-50
Ref.- None

248. **DIAMOND IN CIRCLE**
$2^1/_4$" dia. x $2^1/_2$" ht.
This crude flint mug with pressed handle was probably manufactured around 1860 and is probably English or European. It is known in clear and blue.
Clear $40-50 Blue $80-100
Ref.- None

249. **DOTS IN OVALS**
$2^1/_4$" dia. x $2^1/_2$" ht.
This crude flint mug with pressed handle was probably made about 1860. It is probably English or European. It is known only in turquoise.
Turquoise $80-100
Ref.- None

250. **FINE BLOCK**
$2^1/_2$" dia. x $2^1/_2$" ht.
This flint mug was probably made in England or Europe in the 1860s. It was produced in clear and blue.
Clear $40-50 Blue $80-100
Ref.- None

251. **THREE PANELS OF HOBNAILS**
2" dia. x $2^1/_4$" ht.
This flint mug with pressed handle was probably made about 1860 and was probably English or European. It is known in clear and yellow green.
Clear $40-50 Yellow-Green $80-100
Ref.- None

All of the mugs on this page were probably whiskey tasters.

SCENIC AND WORDS

252. **HOUSE & BOAT MEDALLION**
2 3/4" dia. x 3" ht.
The Iowa City Glass Co. may have made this mug in the 1880s. The shape and handle are identical to Lamb and Lighthouse and is similar to Dog with Collar. It is known in clear only.
Clear $40-45
Ref.- None

253. **NECCO SWEETS**
1 5/8" dia. x 2 1/8" ht.
This mug has a Necco Sweets logo on the front and the word "TRADEMARK" on the back. There are 2 mold variations. The handles are slightly different. It was made only in clear.
Clear $15-20
Ref.- None

254. **DUTCH MILL VARIANT**
not shown
George Davidson & Co. was the maker of this clear mug about 1885. It is marked with their lion's head trademark.
Clear $40-45
Ref.- P&L plate 48

255. **AMERICAN NUT CO.**
1 7/8" dia. x 2 1/2" ht.
This clear mug says, "LOANED BY AMERICAN NUT CO.".On the base it reads, "PEANUT MEASURE".
Clear $15-20
Ref.- None

256. **LIGHTHOUSE**
2" dia. x 2 3/8" ht.
This mug was may have been made by the Iowa City Glass Co. about 1881. The shape and handle are identical to Lamb and House & Boat Medallion and is similar to Dog with Collar. It is known only in clear.
Clear $40-45
Ref.- GCF1 p. 92, TOY p. 138

257. **A. SLAUSEN & CO.**
1 3/8" dia. x 2" ht.
This piece has a 5 pointed star in a circle. Around the star it reads, "A. SLAUSEN & CO., NEW YORK" and "LOZENGE MANUFACTURERS". It was only made in clear.
Clear $15-20
Ref.- None

258. **THOMPSON PHOSPHATE CO.**
1 3/4" dia. x 1 7/8" ht.
This mug is an advertisement for wild cherry made by the Thompson Phosphate Co. Chicago. It was only made in clear.
Clear $15-20
Ref.- None

259. **CASTLE, BOAT & CHURCH MEDALLION**
2 3/4" dia. x 3 1/8" ht.
This mug was probably made about 1880. It was produced in clear and possibly amber and blue.
Clear $40-45 Color $75-90
Ref.- HGC4 p. 33

260. **REMEMBER ME**
3 3/8" dia. x 3 1/2" ht.
This mug was made about 1880 and says "REMEMBER ME". It was produced in clear, amber and cobalt.
Clear $35-40 Amber $45-55 Cobalt $65-80
Ref.- TOY p. 188

261. **HOUSES MEDALLION**
2 3/4" dia. x 3 1/8" ht.
This mug was manufactured about 1880 in clear, amber and blue.
Clear $40-45 Color $75-90
Ref.- None

262. **LIGHTHOUSE & SAILBOAT**
smaller or 2 1/8" dia. x 2 1/4" ht. or 2 3/4" dia. x 3 1/8" ht. or 3 1/4" dia. x 3 5/8" ht.
This mug was probably manufactured in the 1880s. It was made in clear, amber and blue.
All Sizes Clear $30-35 All Sizes Color $45-55
Ref.- GCF1 p. 86, TOY p. 137

263. **DUTCH MILL**
2 3/4" x 2 7/8" ht.
This mug was probably made in the 1880s. It was produced in clear, blue and amethyst.
Clear $40-45 Color $80-100
Ref.- GCF1 p. 82, MET2 p. 205, TOY p. 136

264. **A GOOD BOY**
3" dia. x 3 1/2" ht.
This mug's maker is unknown, but the amber appears to be like that of Atterbury & Co. It was probably made in the 1880s. One side says, "A GOOD BOY", while the other side has a wreath of flowers. It was produced in clear, teal blue, amber and amethyst. There is at least one remake of the mold.
Clear $35-40 Color $40-50
Ref.- GCF1 p. 85, TOY p. 151

265. **A GOOD GIRL**
3" dia. x 3 1/2" ht.
It appears that the maker and date of this pattern is the same as A GOOD BOY. One side says, "A GOOD GIRL", while the other side has a wreath of flowers. It was produced in the same colors.
Clear $35-40 Color $40-50

266. **HAPPY BIRTHDAY (:BUM GEBURTSTAGE)**
2 3/8" dia. x 4" ht.
This flint mug is German, and it wishes the child "happy birthday" in German. Probably made in the 1870s, it is known only in amethyst.
Amethyst $70-90
Ref.- None

267. **PEACE**
3 1/8" dia. x 3" ht.
The word "PEACE" appears on this blue mug in an oval. Probably made by Atterbury & Co. in the 1880s, it is probably a companion piece to "VIRTUE". There is light panelling on the inside. It may have been made in clear and other colors also.
Blue $65-85
Ref.- None

268. **VIRTUE**
2 3/8" dia. x 2 3/8" ht.
This blue mug has the word "VIRTUE" in an oval. The colors in which this mug has been seen are consistant with those produced by Atterbury & Co. It was probably made in the 1880s and appears to be a companion piece to "PEACE". It was made in clear, blue, blue alabaster and possibly in other colors.
Clear $45-55 Color $65-85
Ref.- None

252

253

255

256

257

258

259

260

269. **REMEMBER ME 2**
3 3/8" dia. x 3 3/8" ht.
This dark amber mug reads "REMEMBER ME". It is probably from about 1880.
Amber $45-55
Ref.- None

270. **HIGBEE AD**
2" dia. x 2" ht.
This mug has a bottle on the front that says, "HIGBEE SANITARY BOTTLE". One side reads, "HIGBEE HOT OR COLD SANITARY VACUUM BOTTLE". The other says, "FOR HOME & DOMESTIC USE" and on the left side of that it reads, "KEEPS HOT 48 HOURS" and on the right, "KEEPS COLD 48 HOURS". The bottom reads, "COMPLIMENTS JOHN B. HIGBEE GLASS CO. BRIDGEVILLE, PA". It was made only in clear. The bottle is a very rare item.
Clear $50-60 Bottle $200-250

261

261

264
265

263

266

267

268

269

270

HISTORIC

271

271. **SANDWICH FLUTE**
$4\frac{3}{16}$" ht. and possibly other sizes
This clear flint stein has short flutes around the bottom and is engraved "FRANKIE". It was made to commemorate the birth of Frank Sherman (November 20, 1859) to Andrew and Maria Sherman. The Sherman family had a long association with the Boston & Sandwich Glass Co. This mug was given to the Sandwich Glass Museum with other tableware items engraved with Sherman family names.
Clear $40-50
Ref.- None

272

272. **KNIGHTS OF LABOR**
$2\frac{1}{4}$" dia. x $4\frac{3}{4}$" ht. or $2\frac{3}{4}$" dia. x $5\frac{3}{4}$" ht. or $2\frac{7}{8}$" dia. x $6\frac{1}{2}$" ht.
The Central Glass Co. probably manufactured these steins in the 1870s. An ale glass is shown in PG&B p. 113 (advertisement). The stein reads, "KNIGHTS OF" above the figures and "LABOR" below. This labor union was started in 1869 by Uriah Stephens in Philadelphia. The design has a knight shaking hands with a laborer. These steins were only produced in clear.
All Sizes Clear $80-100
Ref.- AHST p. 515, WHPG p. 157

273

273. **BUMPER TO THE FLAG**
$2\frac{7}{8}$" dia. x $4\frac{1}{8}$" ht.
This flint stein was manufactured by the New England Glass Co. about 1863. One side has a cannon, cannon balls, musket and flag in a large diamond. The other side says, "BUMPER TO THE FLAG" and has a flag, a shield and crossed sabers in a large diamond. The background is covered with a series of smaller diamonds. This stein has been seen with a pewter cover that has an enameled insert with German writing. It was probably a Civil War regimental stein. The regiment's ethnic background was probably Germanic. The stein shown in the Hobbies magazine article has a pewter cover with a sculptured eagle. The stein was made only in clear.
Clear $275-325
With Cover $350-400
Ref.- HOB3

274

274. **E PLURIBUS UNUM**
$2\frac{5}{8}$" dia. x $4\frac{7}{8}$" ht.
This barrel-shaped stein was probably manufactured by Gillinder & Sons in 1876 for the Philadelphia Centennial Exhibition. It says "E PLURIBUS UNUM" and the words are surrounded by stars. It was made only in clear.
Clear $80-100
Ref.- AHST p. 74, AS p. 97, CENT p. 79

275

275. **LIBERTY BELL VARIANT**
$2\frac{5}{8}$" dia. x $4\frac{1}{4}$" ht.
This stein was designed and patented by M. Daniel Connolly on April 27, 1875, and it was made for the Philadelphia Centennial Exhibition in 1876. It was made only in clear. Around the stein it says, "TO PROCLAIM LIBERTY THROUGHOUT ALL THE LAND". Underneath that, it says, "BY ORDER OF THE ASSEMBLY OF PENNA. 1752". On the back it says, "PASS & STOW", "PHILA" and "MDCCLIII".
Clear $100-125
Ref.- PG&B p. 336, WHPG p. 64

276

276. **UNION FOREVER**
$3\frac{1}{4}$" dia. x $4\frac{1}{8}$" ht.
This flint stein was probably manufactured by either the Boston & Sandwich Glass Co. or the New England Glass Co. about 1863. It may have been made to help improve morale during the Civil

277

278

279

280

281

War. One side says, "UNION FOREVER" over clasped hands which are over a document that says, "CONSTITUTION". The other side reads, "BUMPER TO THE FLAG" and has a flag, a shield and crossed sabers. It was only produced in clear. This design is also known on 3 tumbler sizes.
Clear $275-325
Ref.- AHST p. 485, AS p. 241, MET2 p. 6

277. **CENTENNIAL SHIELD**
probably smaller or 2 1/2" dia. x 5 1/4" ht.
This stein was manufactured by the Central Glass Co. for the Philadelphia Centennial Exhibition in 1876. It was made only in clear.
Clear $110-135
Ref.- HOB4

278. **CENTENNIAL STAR**
2" dia. x 4 1/2" ht. or 2 1/2" dia. x 5 1/4" ht.
This stein was manufactured by the Central Glass Co. for the Philadelphia Centennial Exhibition in 1876. It was made only in clear.
Both Sizes Clear $100-125
Ref.- PG&B p. 111 (patent drawing), CENT p. 80

279. **CENTENNIAL STAR BAND**
2 5/8" dia. x 4 5/8" ht. or
3 1/4" dia. x 5 1/4" ht.
These steins were made by Hobbs, Brockunier & Co. for the Philadelphia Centennial Exhibition in 1876. One variation has the word "Centennial" around the base, while the other variation bears the words "Liberty & Republic". George B. Fowle from Cambridge, Ma. designed and patented this stein on April 11, 1876. The "Cenntenial" stein was produced in clear. The "Liberty and Republic" stein was made in amber and teal blue in the larger size. It seems likely that these steins were also made in other colors and clear.
Both Sizes "Centennial" Clear $100-125 Large "Liberty and Republic" Color $200-250
Ref.- HOB3 p. 99, PG&B p. 190 (advertisement), WHPG p. 64

280. **COLUMBIAN COIN**
2 3/4" dia. x 4 3/4" ht.
The pattern was manufactured after March of 1892 by the U. S. Glass Co. at factory "N". This pattern replaced American Coin when the government stopped its production. Items always have an obverse and a reverse of a coin. The obverse has either a bust of Columbus, a bust of Americus Vespucius or an eagle. The reverse has any one of the following coats of arms: American or 4 Spanish variations. The pattern was made in clear, with gold, acid frosted and opaque white. Over 30 different items were made in this pattern.
Clear $150-175
Ref.- WHPG p. 72 (mug not listed)

281. **AMERICAN COIN (SILVER AGE, U. S. GLASS' NO. 15005)**
2 3/4" dia. x 4 3/4" ht.
A stein is shown. This pattern was made from February to March of 1892 by the U. S. Glass Co. The U. S. Treasury Department stopped production because the law prohibited reproducing U. S. currency. Real coins were used in the molds. The mug has the obverse and the reverse of the silver dollar. The pattern was produced in clear, acid frosted and is rare ruby stained. Over 45 different items were made in this pattern. There are items in the pattern that have been reproduced, but the mug has not.
Clear $300-375 Frosted $400-500
Ref.- AHST p. 94, KM7 p. 105 (advertisement), LEEV p. 39, MET1 p. 113

282. **KNIGHTS OF LABOR / ARBITRATION**
3" dia. x 7" ht. not shown
This stein was probably made in the 1870s. It has a man in a frock and top hat (probably represents the employer) shaking hands with a laborer. It says, "ARBITRATION" below the figures. It was made only in clear.
Clear $80-100
Ref.- AHST p. 515, MET2 p. 188, WHPG p. 157

283

284

285

286

287

288

283. **DANDELION / KNIGHTS TEMPLAR**
3 1/2" dia. x 3 5/8" ht.
The Knight's Templar insignia is on the base of this mug, and it is dated "MAY 27, 28, 29, 1912". The pattern was manufactured by the H. Northwood Co. of Wheeling, West Virginia. It was made in marigold carnival and ice blue carnival.
Carnival Colors $1000+
Ref.- CARN p. 58, HCG3 p. 18

284. **EAGLE DRUM**
2 5/8" dia. x 2 1/4" ht.
The Westmoreland Specialty Co. manufactured this mug starting about 1909. The retail price was 15 cents. It was made in clear with gold, opaque white with gold and ruby stained with the words, "50th ANNIVERSARY BATTLE OF GETTYSBURG 1863-1913". Some have a tin cover with a slot to be used as a bank. Another variation of this mug has an "R" inside a keystone. It is tan and clear slag and was made about the same date.
Clear $25-30 Stain $45-55
Ref.- TOY p. 152

285. **TENNESSEE ROSE**
3 1/8" dia. x 3 3/8" ht.
This acid frosted mug has a Cherokee Rose in a medallion on one side and an American flag with 16 stars on the other. The rose medallion and the flag are painted red, gold and blue. The mug was made in 1897 to celebrate the centennial of Tennessee's admission to statehood.
Clear $45-55
add 50% for good paint
Ref.- AHST p. 113, AS p. 73, WHPG p. 261

286. **SHRINE, LION WITH FLAG**
4" dia. x 5 1/4" ht.
This rare mug was probably manufactured in the 1880s. It is known in opaque white and opaque blue, usually painted a dull gold. The front has a lion in high relief under a moon and star. Each side has crossed flags with a moon and star on each flag and between the crossed flags. There are 15 panels. This mug is probably a companion piece to the Lion Hunt mug.
Opaque Blue $225-275
Opaque White $175-225
Ref.- None

287. **AL KORAN TEMPLE SHRINE**
3 1/2" dia. x 4 3/8" ht.
This mug, which has an applied handle, says, "AL KORAN TEMPLE", "CLEVELAND", "SEPT,25 1913" and "WILLIAM M. BOGUE, POTENTATE". It has gold and white decoration.
Decorated $70-90
REF.- None

288. **GARFIELD SHAVING MUG**
3 3/8" dia. x 2 5/8" ht.
Atterbury & Co. probably made this mug in 1881 after the assassination of President Garfield. The blue alabaster is identical to that used in other known Atterbury glass. This mug is rare in opaque white and extremely rare in blue alabaster. The mug has a small oval bowl to hold the shaving brush and a large bowl for soap. One side has a bust of Garfield surrounded by ivy, while the other side has his wife surrounded by laurel.
Opaque White $200-250
Blue Alabaster $600-700
REF.- AHST p. 309 MG p. 112

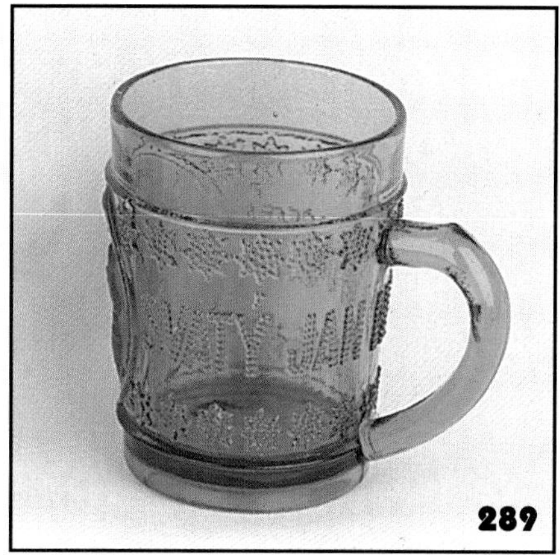
289

290

291

292

293

294

289. **ST. JOHN (SVATY JAN NEPOMACY)**
2 3/8" dia. x 3 1/8" ht.
This mug was probably made in Czechoslovakia about 1900. The front has a frosted picture of St. John carrying a cross and holding an olive branch. Beaded letters say, "SVATY JAN NEPOMACY". It is known only in blue, but was probably made in clear also.
Blue $55-65
Ref.- None

290. **CLEVELAND & THURMOND**
3" dia. x 3 1/8" ht.
This rare mug was made for the presidential campaign of 1888. A bust of Cleveland appears on one side and a bust of Thurmond on the other. It was produced in clear, amber and blue. The opposing candidates, Harrison and Morton, also had a mug.
Clear $125-150 Color $250-300
Ref.- AHST p. 331, AS p. 335

291. **HARRISON & MORTON**
3" dia. x 3 1/8" ht.
This rare mug was made for the presidential campaign of 1888. There is a bust of Harrison on one side and a bust of Morton on the other. It was produced in clear, amber and blue. The opposing candidates, Cleveland and Thurmond, also had a mug.
Clear $125-150 Color $250-300
Ref.- AHST p. 329, AS p. 334

292. **SHRINE, FISH HANDLE**
2 3/4" dia. x 3 3/8" ht.
The Westmoreland Specialty Co. made this enameled mug. On one side, it says "PITTSBURGH, PA." and has a girl holding a sword that says "SYRIA" with a moon and star hanging from it. The other side says "ATLANTIC CITY July 13, 1904" and has a sailboat. The handle is a fish.
Clear $80-100
Ref.- None

293. **SHRINE, INDIAN**
2 5/8" dia. x 3 3/8" ht.
The Westmoreland Specialty Co. was the maker of this enameled mug. On each side of the handle this mug says "PITTSBURGH" in a moon with an Egyptian face and is dated 1903 in a star hanging from the moon. The front has an Indian with a headdress. There are tomahawks and a pipe. "SARA" and "TOGA" are on each side and under the bust. The handle is a sword with the word "SYRIA" on it.
Clear $80-100
Ref.- None

294. **SHRINE, FLOWER**
3 1/4" dia. x 2 3/8" ht.
The Westmoreland Specialty Co. was the manufacturer of this clear cup and saucer with enameling. The cup is an orange flower with a green stem handle. The bottom reads "SYRIA" and "PITTSBURGH". The saucer has a sword with a moon and star hanging from it. "SYRIA" is on the sword and each side of the moon reads "PITTS" and "BURGH". Across from this decoration are the words "LOS ANGELES MAY 1906". There are free form enameled flowers at 90° to the rest of the decoration. The cup is shown in a 1912 Westmoreland Specialty Catalogue.
Clear $80-100
50% less without saucer
Ref.- None

295

297

297

296

298

299

300

301

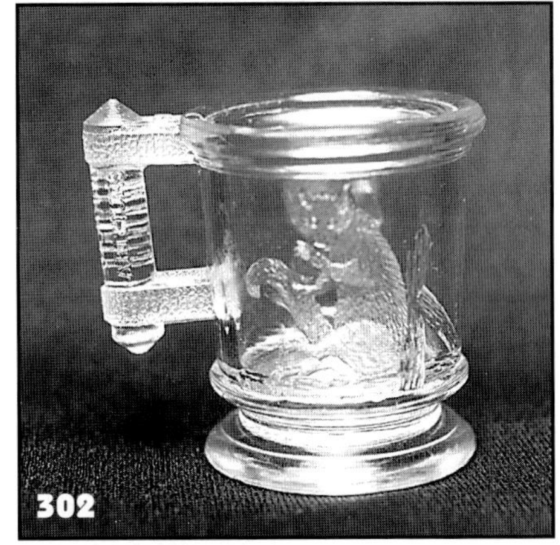
302

303

304

304

305

307

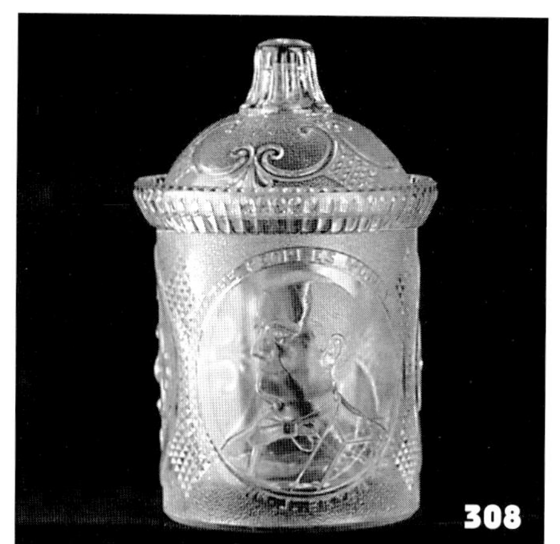
308

309

310

311

312

313

314

315

316

317

295. **INDEPENDENCE HALL**
3" dia. x 3 1/4" ht.
This mug may have been manufactured by the Boston & Sandwich Glass Co. in 1876 for the Philadelphia Centennial Exhibition. It has the same base and handle as "Plain Dodecagon Bottom" which has a Sandwich history, except the base says "INDEPENDENCE HALL" and shows that building. It was made only in clear and as an etched souvenir.
Clear $90-110
Ref.- CORN p. 289, HOB2

296. **PLAIN DODECAGON BOTTOM**
3" dia. x 3 1/4" ht.
This mug is engraved with the initials, "M. E. K." which probably stands for Mary Elizabeth Kern. The mug has been passed down through the Kern family. Mary was the granddaughter of Francis Kern (1813-1884), who was the foreman in the Boston & Sandwich Glass Co. cutting room for many years. This mug is in the Sandwich Glass Museum collection.
Clear $40-50
Ref. - None

297. **PLAIN DODECAGON BOTTOM VARIANT**
2 1/2" dia. x 3 1/8" ht.
These mugs have "C" shaped handle and may be a mold variation of the Sandwich mug listed above. Some of these mugs have been engraved with the date 1876. Another variation has "CENTENNIAL 1876" pressed in the bottom.
Clear $40-50 Clear with 1876 Bottom $80-100
Ref. - None

298. **GLADSTONE**
2 1/2" dia. x 2 1/2" ht.
The Wear Flint Glass Co. made this pattern. The pieces say, "GLADSTONE FOR THE MILLION". They also have an English rose, a Scottish thistle and an Irish shamrock. They were made to honor William Ewart Gladstone (1809-1898), who was Prime Minister of England 4 times. There is a creamer and a bowl, as well as the cup and saucer. The pattern was made in clear, blue and amethyst.
Clear $125-150 Color $200-250 50% less without saucer
Ref.- AHST p. 450, ENG p. 95, ENGP p. 77 & 139, WHPG p. 125

299. **PEABODY**
2 1/2" dia. x 2 1/2" ht.
The Wear Flint Glass Co. was the maker of this pattern. The registry mark deates from July 31, 1869. George Peabody (1795-1869) was a well known philanthropist in England and the United States. There is a creamer and a bowl as well as the cup and saucer. They were made in clear, blue and amethyst.
Clear $100-150 Color $200-250 50% less without saucer
Ref.- AHST p. 382, CORN p. 365, ENG p. 95, WHPG p. 199

300. **ROWING CHAMPION**
3" dia. x 4 1/8" ht.
This mug was manufactured by the Wear Flint Glass Co. The registry mark is for Dec. 8, 1888. The front shows a picture of a man sitting in a boat. Over the picture are the words, "EDWARD HANLAN CHAMPION OF THE WORLD NOV 15, 1888". Underneath it says, "BEAT TRICETT OF N.S.W.". There are crossed oars on each side. It was produced in clear and opalescent.
Clear $70-90 Opalescent $125-150
Ref.- ENG p. 99, SW2

301. **HAYES & WHEELER**
1 3/4" dia. x 2" ht.
Adams & Co. manufactured this mug for the presidential campaign of 1876. It is a varation of the Liberty Bell pattern mug. The name "HAYES" is on the bell on one side, while the name "WHEELER" is on the bell on the other. A ribbon between the bells has the dates "1776-1876". The base says, "ADAMS & CO. GLASS WORKS". It was made in clear and opaque white and both are rare.
Clear $200-250
Opaque White $400-500
Ref.- AHST p. 301, AS p. 289

302. **GARFIELD & ARTHUR**
1 7/8" dia. x 2 1/4" ht.
This mug was made for the presidential campaign of 1880. One side of the mug has a bust of Garfield with his name underneath, while the other side has a raccoon (symbol of the Republican Party at this time) thumbing its nose. The date "1880" is on top of the handle, while the names "GARFIELD" & "ARTHUR" are on each side. The lip of the base is plain. The bottom reads, "ADAMS & CO. GLASS MFGRS." It was produced in clear and cobalt is rare.
Clear $160-200 Cobalt $500-600
Ref.- AHST p. 303, AS p. 311

303. **McKINLEY, PROTECTION & PLENTY**
8 oz.
McKee Brothers & Co. made this mug for the presidential campaign of 1896. It shows McKinley in a shield with stars and the words, "PROTECTION AND PLENTY" beneath it. It was made in clear and with gold.
Clear $80-100
Ref.- HCO p. 96 (advertisement)

304. **LIBERTY BELL WITH SNAKE**
3 3/8" dia. x 3 5/8" ht.
Gillinder & Sons made this mug on site at the Philadelphia Centennial Exhibition in 1876. "MANUFACTURED BY GILLINDER & SONS AT THE CENTENNIAL EXHIBITION" is impressed on the base. The bowl is an inverted Liberty Bell and the handle is a snake. It was produced in clear and opaque white.
Clear and Opaque White $450-500
Ref.- JLPG p. 324, LEE p. 344, MMPG p. 504

305. **HIGH LEVEL BRIDGE**
3 1/4" dia. x 3 7/8" ht.
This flint mug with pressed handle was probably manufactured in England about 1850. It has a bridge completely around the mug. A train is on the bridge. Above the bridge, it says, "HIGH LEVEL BRIDGE NEWCASTLE ON TYNE". Between the front and the first trestle to the left it says "COMMENCED APRIL 24 1846". Then, between the front and the first trestle to the right it says, "OPENED JANUY 16 1850". The glass is of rather poor quality, and it is known only in clear.
Clear $75-100
Ref.- ENGP p. 139

306. **CABLE**
p. 147 for pattern picture
Boston & Sandwich Glass Co. was the manufacturer of this flint pattern from about 1858. That was the date that the first Trans-Atlantic cable was completed, however, it was unsuccessful. This pattern was issued to commemorate that event. The mug is made from a whiskey tumbler and has an applied handle. The pattern was produced in clear and is rare in color. Over 30 different pieces were made in it.
Clear $175-225
Ref.- JLPG p. 100, LEE p. 181

307. **GOAT REARING**
possibly smaller or 2 3/8" dia. x 3 3/8" ht. or 2 3/4" dia. x 4 3/8"
This flint stein was probably made in the 1870s or 80s. A man with a stein is kicking a rearing goat in the stomach. The significance of the design is not known, but we've been told it is I.O.O.F. (Odd Fellows) related. The bottom of the stein says, "PATT APPLYD FOR". It was made only in clear
Both Sizes $80-100
Ref.- None

308. **BRYAN, COVERED**
3 1/4" dia. x 3 1/2" ht.
McKee & Brothers was the maker of this covered mug for the Presidential campaign of 1896. The front of the mug has a bust of Bryan with his name, "Wm. J. BRYAN", underneath. Above the bust it says, "THE PEOPLES MONEY". It was made only in clear. The opposing candidate, Wm. McKinley, also had a covered mug.
Clear $70-85 without cover 50% less
Ref.- AHST p. 339, AS p. 351

309. **McKINLEY, COVERED**
3 1/4" dia. x 3 1/2" ht.
McKee & Brothers manufactured this covered mug for the presidential campaign of 1896. The front of the mug has a bust of McKinley with his name, "MAJ. Wm. McKINLEY", underneath. Above the bust it says, "PROTECTION AND PLENTY". It was made only in clear. The opposing candidate, Wm. J. Bryan, also had a covered mug.
Clear $70-85 without cover 50% less
Ref.- AHST p. 339, AS p. 351

310. **SHRINE**
2 1/4" dia. x 3 1/2" ht.
This pattern was manufactured by the Beatty-Brady Glass Co. about 1896. It is shown in the Baltimore Bargain House catalogues for 1903 and 1904, and it is also shown in a 1907-08 Indiana Glass Co. catalogue. The pattern has beaded moons and stars on every other panel and beaded teardrops on the remaining panels. It was only produced in clear. There are about 20 different pieces in the pattern.
Clear $35-40
Ref.- HCP3 p. 6 (advertisement, but no mug), GREE plate 277, JLPG p. 480 (mug not listed)

311. **GARFIELD MEMORIAL**
1 7/8" dia. x 2 1/4" ht.
Adams & Co. was the maker of this mug which was made to commemorate the assassination death of the American President, James Garfield. It is a remake of the Garfield-Arthur presidential campaign mug. One side of this mug has a bust of Garfield with "JAMES A. GARFIELD" underneath it. The other side is draped with the dates of his birth (NOV 19th 1831), assassination (JULY 2nd 1881) and death (SEPT 19th 1881). The lip of the base has beads, and the bottom has an blank center. The date 1880 is on top of the handle, as it was on the campaign mug. Obviously, it was overlooked in the remake of the mug. It was made in clear and is rare in amber.
Clear $90-110 Amber $300-400
Ref.- AHST p. 303, AS p. 312, TOY p. 141

312. **GARFIELD & LINCOLN**
2 5/8" dia. x 2 5/8" ht.
Adams & Co. manufactured this mug in 1881 to commemorate the deaths of the assassinated American Presidents, Abraham Lincoln and James Garfield. One side of the mug has a bust of Lincoln and the other a bust of Garfield with their names underneath. To the left of each bust are their birth dates, to the right the dates of their assassinations; underneath each bust is the date that each man died along with their last names. The bottom of the mug says "OUR COUNTRYS MARTYRS". It was produced in clear and is rare in cobalt.
Clear $70-90 Cobalt $300-400
Ref.- AHST p. 287, AS p. 219, WHPG p. 22

313. **FRANZ JOSEPH**
2 1/8" dia. x 3 3/8" ht.
This mug was probably made in Europe and is dated "1848-1898". It has the bust of Franz Joseph of Austria-Hungary and was made to celebrate his 50th anniversary as Emperor. The overall design of the mug is the same as the Stars & Stripes pattern, except this mug is barrel shaped. It was produced in clear and blue.
Clear $45-55 Blue $60-75
Ref.- None

314. **LIBERTY BELL**
1 3/4" dia. x 2" ht.
The Oct. 28, 1875 issue of the Crockery and Glass Journal attributes this pattern to Adams & Co. It was designed and patented by James C. Gill on Sept. 28, 1875. The mug has a Liberty Bell on each side and the inscription, "1776-1876" on a ribbon between the bells. It was produced in clear. The mug and the platter were made in opaque white. There are over 35 different items in this pattern.
Clear $100-125
Opaque White $150-175
Ref.- CENT p. 79, CLUB, JLPG p. 324, OPA plate 222, TOY p. 151

315. **COLUMBUS**
2 5/8" dia. x 2 1/2" ht.
The Novelty Glass Co. of Fostoria, Oh. was the maker of this mug in 1892. The mug has a bust of Columbus with the dates 1492 and 1892 on each side. It is known in clear, etched, and with gold. A rare saucer that matches the mug has been seen.
Clear $65-75 Good Gold $90-110 add 100% for the saucer
Ref.- AHST p. 4, FOS p. 41

316. **COLUMBUS & WASHINGTON**
2 1/2" dia. x 2 5/8" ht.
This mug shows Columbus on one side and Washington on the other. The base is marked, "WORLDS COLUMBIAN EXPOSITION 1893". It was only produced in clear.
Clear $90-110
Ref.- AHST p. 4, AS p. 6

317. **COLUMBUS LANDING**
2 1/2" dia. x 2 5/8" ht.
This mug shows Columbus' flagship, the Santa Maria on one side and Columbus and his men raising a flag on the other. The base is marked, "WORLDS FAIR 1893". It was only produced in clear.
Clear $90-110
Ref.- AHST p. 4, AS p. 6

A variant of *316* and *317* has been reported, that has a bust of Columbus on one side and the ship on the other.

BEADS

318

319

318. **BEADED BANDS**
3 1/8" dia. x 3 5/8" ht.
This mug has an applied handle and is probably from the 1870s. It is known only in clear.
Clear $35-40
Ref.- None

319. **WISCONSIN (BEADED DEWDROP, U. S. GLASS' NO. 15079)**
mug: 2 3/4" dia. x 3 7/8" ht. or cup and saucer
The pattern was produced by the U. S. Glass Co. about 1898. It was made in clear only. There are about 80 different items in the pattern.
Clear Mug $40-50
Clear Cup and Saucer $50-60
50% less without saucer
Ref.- JLPG p. 560, LEE p. 243, MET1 p. 189, MMPG p. 314, WHPG p. 33

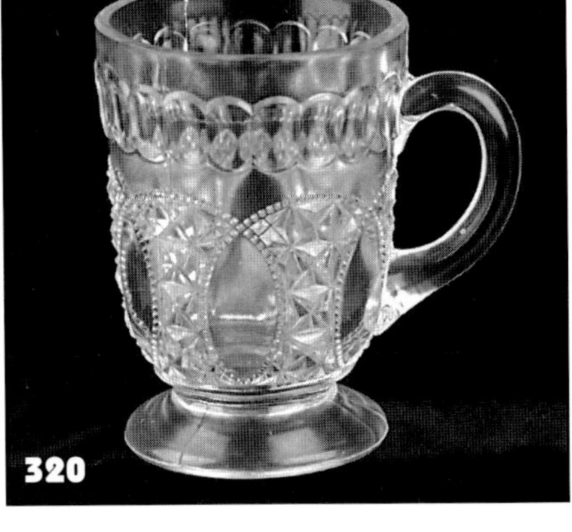
320

321

320. **OREGON (BEADED OVALS, U. S. GLASS' NO. 15073)**
2 3/4" dia. x 3 7/8" ht.
This pattern was manufactured by the U. S. Glass Co. about 1907. It was made in clear. It is rare in green and ruby stain. There are about 60 different pieces in the pattern.
Clear $35-40
Green and Stain $75-100
Ref.- JLPG p. 392, MMPG p. 238, WHPG p. 35

321. **CORD DRAPERY (NATIONAL's No. 350)**
2 3/8" dia. x 3 1/8" ht.
The National Glass Co. (at the Indiana Tumbler & Goblet Works) manufactured this pattern from 1900 to June, 1903, when the plant burned. It was also shown in a 1907-08 Indiana Glass Co. catalogue. The pattern was made in clear, amber, blue, blue-green, canary, emerald green, milk glass, chocoalte and possibly nile green.
Clear $45-55 Amber, Blue-Green and Blue $150-175
Ref.- GRE p. 60, GREE plate 277

322. **DEWDROP**
3" dia. x 3 1/2" ht.
This non-flint mug has an early type applied handle and was probably made in the 1870s. The pattern was produced in clear, amber, blue and canary.
Clear $35-40 Color $65-80
Ref.- MET1 p. 191 (mug not listed)

322

323. **INVERTED HOBNAIL ARCHES**
2 5/8" dia. x 3 3/8" ht.
Dalzell, Gilmore & Leighton Co. made this clear mug from about 1884 to 1895.
Clear $35-40
Ref.- FIN p. 116

323

324. **WASHINGTON, STATE SERIES (U. S. GLASS' NO. 15074)**
2 3/4" dia. x 2 7/8" ht.
The U. S. Glass Co. manufactured this pattern about 1907. It was made in clear, blue, light green, turquoise and ruby stain. The ruby stained items are often souvenired. Over 30 different items were made in the pattern.
Clear $20-25
Color and Stain $35-40
Ref.- HC7 p. 213 (mug not listed)

325. **TINY THUMBPRINT**
custard cup or mug:
2 3/4" dia. x 2 7/8" ht.
The Tarentum Glass Co. was the maker of this pattern in the early 1900s. It was produced in clear, green, green custard, yellow custard and ruby stain. There are about 20 different pieces in the pattern.
Clear $20-30
Color and Stain Custard $20-25
Color and Stain Mug $30-35
Ref.- TAR p. 344

326. **COLORADO (LACY MEDALLION, U. S. GLASS' NO. 15057)**
cup: Small or 2 7/8" dia. x 2 3/4" ht.
footed or mug: 2 1/8" dia. x 2 3/8" ht. or
2 5/8" dia. x 2 3/4" ht. or
2 7/8" dia. x 3 3/4" ht.
The U. S. Glass Co. was the maker of these mugs and cups about 1898. The cup is a custard. The pattern is only called Lacy Medallion when it is souvenired. The mugs and cups were made in clear, green, blue, clambroth and ruby stain. The pattern includes about 60 different items.
All Sizes in Clear and Green $25-35
All Sizes in Clambroth $35-45
All Sizes Blue and Stain $45-55
Ref.- HC5 p. 149 (advertisement),
JLPG p. 126, MMPG p. 88
A&C2 p.232 (advertisement)

327. **BEADED OVALS WITH PLEATED SKIRT**
2" dia. x 3 1/4" ht.
This stein was probably made in the 1880s. It was made in clear, green, amber and blue.
Clear $20-25 Color $35-40
Ref.- GCF1 p. 89

328. **BEADED ARCH PANELS**
2 1/2" dia. x 2 5/8" ht. or
2 5/8" dia. x 3 1/2" ht.
The Burlington Glass Works was the maker of this mug about 1890. It was made in clear and blue.
Both Sizes Clear $20-25
Both Sizes Blue $40-50
Ref.- TOY p. 141, MMPG p. 68,
WHPG p. 31

329. **BEADED SHELL (NEW YORK)**
2 7/8" dia. x 3 3/4" ht.
This pattern was first manufactured by the Dugan Glass Co. in 1904. It was produced in, clear, green and blue (the colors typically deocrated with gold) as well as clear opalescent, light green opalescent and blue opalescent. Later, carnival colors were made: amethyst, blue, white (rare) and marigold. The pattern was made in berry sets, water sets, table sets, and condiment sets as well as mugs. A reproduction mug in custard was distributed by L. G. Wright; it has a lazy "N" on the bottom.
Blue and Marigold $150-175
Amethyst $90-110
Horehound $275-325 White $700+
Ref.- HCG2 p. 12 (no picture),
CARN p. 20 and 8 (price guide)

330. **DART & BALL**
1 1/2" dia. x 1 7/8" ht.
This mug was probably made after 1900. It was produced in clear and cobalt.
Clear $15-20 Cobalt $30-40
Ref.- GCF1 p. 93

331. **BEAD & SCROLL**
2 1/4" dia. x 3 1/4" ht. or
2 3/4" dia. x 3 1/4" ht.
The maker of this pattern was the U. S. Glass Co. about 1901. It was produced in clear, amber, blue, green (with a yellowish tint), cobalt, frosted and ruby stain. It was a popular souvenir item for the 1901 Pan American Exposition. Over 35 different pieces were made in this pattern.
Both Sizes Clear $25-30 Both Sizes Amber and Green $35-40 Both Sizes Amber and Green $45-55 add 25% for Pan-American Exposition
Ref.- WHPG p. 31

324

325

326

327

328

329

330

331

331

332

328

334

335

336

CIRCLES

332. **BULLSEYE & FAN (U. S. GLASS' NO. 15090)**
3 1/8" dia. x 5 1/4" ht.
This item is called a lemonade because of the tall, slender shape. It was made by the U. S. Glass Co. about 1905. It was produced in clear, with gold and with stained bullseyes. The stain colors are blue, green and rose.
Clear $20-25 Good Gold and Stain $30-35
Ref.- MMPG p. 74

333. **CURRIER & IVES (EULALIA)**
2 1/2" dia. x 2 7/8" ht.
The Bellaire Goblet Co. and the Cooperative Flint Glass Co. were the makers of this pattern in the 1890s. The items of interest are a cup and saucer. The pattern was made in clear, amber, blue and opaque white. The table service is extensive and includes a water and a wine tray with a "balky mule on the railroad tracks". There are about 35 different items in this pattern.
Clear $60-75 Color $125-150 50% less without saucer
Ref.- JLPG p. 143, MET1 p. 159, MMPG p. 18

334. **MULTIPLE SCROLL (CANTON NO. 130)**
2 1/4" dia. x 3" ht.
The Canton Glass Co. was the maker of this pattern in the late 1880s. It was produced in clear, amber and blue.
Clear $20-25 Color $35-40
Ref.- KM6 plate 27 (advertisement - but no mug)

335. **THOUSAND EYE**
1 3/4" dia. x 2" ht. or 2 1/8" dia. x 2 1/2" ht. or 2 5/8" dia. x 3 3/8" ht.
Adams & Co. was the maker of this pattern in the 1870s and 80s. The U. S. Glass Co. made it after 1891. It may have also been made at the Burlington Glass Works. It was produced in clear, amber, blue, apple green, canary and opalescent colors. Over 70 different items were manufactured in this pattern.
All Sizes Clear $20-25
All Sizes Color $25-30
Ref.- JLPG p. 516, LEE p. 506, MET1 p. 185

336. **THREE PANEL (RICHARDS & HARTLEY'S NO. 25)**
2 1/2" dia. x 3" ht. or 3" dia. x 3 3/8" ht.
The Richards & Hartley Flint Glass Co. made this pattern about 1890. Another possible maker was the Burlington Glass Works. It was made in clear, amber, blue and canary. There are over 25 different pieces in the pattern.
Both Sizes Clear $20-25
Both Sizes Color $30-40
Ref.- HC5 p. 113 (advertisement), JLPG p. 520, PG&B p. 286 (advertisement), MMPG p. 66, TAR p. 244, TOY p. 139, WHPG p. 265

337. **DIAMOND POINT DISCS**
3" dia. x 3 1/4" ht.
Bryce, Higbee & Co. manufactured this pattern about 1898. After 1907, it was made by the J. B. Higbee Glass Co. Then, after 1919, it was made by the New Martinsville Glass Mfg. Co. It was produced in clear, ruby stain and with gold.
Clear $20-25 Stain $40-50
Ref.- HC7 p. 105 (mug not listed)

338. **STAR IN BULLSEYE (U. S. GLASS' NO. 15092)**
3" dia. x 2 7/8" ht.
The U. S. Glass Co. was the maker of this pattern about 1905. The pattern is shown in a New Martinsville Glass Mfg. Co. catalogue from about 1918. A punch cup or a custard is shown. It was produced in clear, with gold, ruby stain and rose stain. There are over 30 different items in the pattern.
Clear $10-15 Stain $20-25
Ref.- JLPG p. 455, MET1 125, PG&B p. 86, WEPG p. 435 NM p.29 (advertisement)

339. **KNURLED DOT BAND**
2 3/8" dia. x 3 5/8" ht.
This mug was shown in a 1907-08 Indiana Glass Co. catalogue. It was only produced in clear.
Clear $25-30
Ref.- GREE plate 277

340. **PANELLED HOB**
2 3/8" dia. x 3" ht.
This clear mug was manufactured by the Co-Operative Flint Glass Co. about 1910. In their catalogue it is called a 4 oz. mug.
Clear $20-25
Ref.- COOP

341. **PRISM & BALL**
2" dia. x 2 5/8" ht.
This mug was probably made in the early 1900s. It is known in clear as well as a souvenir with enameled flowers.
Clear $20-25
Ref.- None

342. **BURRED DISC & FAN**
2 7/8" dia. x 3 7/8" ht.
This mug with an applied handle was probably made about 1900. It is known only in clear.
Clear $25-30
Ref.- None

343. **CANDLEWICK (BANDED RAINDROPS)**
2 3/4" dia. x 3 1/4" ht.
This pattern was probably produced in the 1890s. It was made in clear and opaque white.
Clear $40-50 Opaque White $55-65
50% less without saucer
Ref.- WHPG p. 26

344. **O. K.**
1 1/2" dia. x 1 1/2" ht.
This small Hobnail mug was made in clear after 1900, probably as a scoop for penny candy. The medallion says, "O K".
Clear $10-15
Ref.- None

345. **BEADED THUMBPRINT BLOCK**
2 7/8" dia. x 3 7/8" ht.
The tumbler has an applied handle and was manufactured by the U. S. Glass Co. about 1893. It was produced in clear and probably ruby stain.
Clear $25-30
Ref.- HC7 p. 74 (mug not listed)

346. **HOBNAIL, 7 ROWS**
2 3/4" dia. x 3" ht.
A. J. Beatty & Sons made this mug in the 1880s. After 1891, it was made by the U. S. Glass Co. It is known in clear.
Clear $20-25
Ref.- HOB1, PG&B p. 58 (advertisement)

337

338

339

340

341

342

343

344

345

346

347

348

349

350

351

347. **PRINTED HOBNAIL**
$2^3/_4$" dia. x $2^7/_8$" ht.
This mug was made in the late 1800s. It is occasionally found with slotted cover to make it a mustard. It was produced in clear, amber, blue, green, canary and amethyst.
Clear $20-25 Color $30-35
add 50% for cover
Ref.- LEE p. 277, MMPG p. 66

348. **HOBNAIL IN SQUARE (VESTA, AETNA'S NO. 335 1/2)**
$2^1/_2$" dia. x $3^1/_8$" ht.
Aetna Glass & Manufacturing Co. was the maker of this pattern about 1887. It was made in clear, amber, blue, apple green, opalescent and canary.
Clear $30-35 Color $45-55
Ref.- KM5 plate 24 (advertisement - but no mug), MET2 p. 99 (mug not listed)

349. **DOUBLE EYE HOBNAIL WITH BAND (DEW DROP)**
mug or cup and saucer:
$2^3/_4$" dia. x $2^3/_8$" ht.
The Columbia Glass Co. was the maker of this pattern about 1887. It was made in clear, amber and blue.
Both Clear $35-45
Both Color $60-75 50% less without saucer
Ref.- FIN p. 65 and 29 (advertisement), FINP p. 56, GCF1 p. 50, HC5 p. 130 (advertisement), LEE plate 82, MMPG p. 308, PG&B p. 58 and 126 (advertisements)

350. **HOBNAIL**
many sizes and shapes
This pattern was made by many manufacturers including the Bryce Brothers, Gillinder & Sons, McKee & Brother and the U. S. Glass Co. Other Hobnail manufacturers are listed elsewhere with the specific type of Hobnail that they manufactured. Hobnail was produced in many colors.
Clear $15-30 Color $25-50
Ref.- FINP p. 56, KM7 p. 109 (advertisement), LEE p. 259, MET1 p. 187, PG&B p. 58 (advertisement), TOY p. 137

351. **CRESTED HOBNAIL**
$2^1/_2$" dia. x $3^1/_8$" ht.
This mug was manufactured by A. J. Beatty & Sons about 1887. It sometimes has a cover with a notched hole to convert it into a mustard. It was produced in clear, amber and blue.
Clear $20-25 Color $30-35
add 50% for cover
Ref.- GCF2 p. 202, TOY p. 156

350

350

350

352

353

354

355

356

357

358

359

360

352. **BARRED HOBNAIL**
2 1/2" dia. x 3" ht.
The Brilliant Glass Works produced this pattern in a limited table service about 1888. It was made in clear, amber, possibly in blue and frosted in all colors.
Clear $25-30
Amber $35-45
Ref.- GCF1 p. 84, MET1 p. 187

353. **THE STATES (CANE AND STAR MEDALLION, U. S. GLASS' NO. 15093)**
2 3/4" dia. x 2 1/4" ht.
This pattern was manufactured by the U. S. Glass Co. about 1905. A punch cup is show, and there is also a punch bowl. The pattern was produced in clear and green, and over 35 different pieces were made.
Clear $10-15 Green $15-20
Ref.- HC5 p. 152 (advertisement), MMPG p. 90

354. **CAROLINA (INVERNESS, U. S. GLASS' NO. 15083)**
2 3/4" dia. x 3 7/8" ht.
This mug was manufactured by Bryce Brothers in the 1880s and the U. S. Glass Co. took over production after 1891. The convex thumbprints are on the inside. It was made in clear, ruby stain and purple stain.
Clear $25-30 Stain $35-40
Ref.- JLPG p. 110

355. **PUNTY BAND (HEISEY'S NO. 1220)**
2 5/8" dia. x 3 3/8" ht.
The A. H. Heisey Glass Co. was the maker of this pattern between 1897 and 1910. It was made in clear, custard, opaque white and ruby stain. The pattern has over 30 different items.
Clear $20-25 Color $35-45
Ref.- HSY p. 53, MMPG p. 42

356. **HOBNAIL WITH NOTCHED HANDLE**
2 1/2" dia. x 3" ht.
Doyle & Co. manufactured this mug in the 1880s. After 1891, production continued with the U. S. Glass Co. Hobs cover the bottom of the mug. Sometimes a slotted cover is used to make this mug a mustard. It was produced in clear, amber, amethyst and blue.
Clear $20-25
Color $30-35 add 50% for cover
Ref.- GCF2 p. 202, WEPG p. 354

357. **BURRED HOBNAIL**
2 5/8" dia. x 2 3/4" ht.
The Canton Glass Co. manufactured this pattern in the 1880s. The pattern size is limited to a few items. It was made in clear, blue, opaque blue and opaque white.
Clear $25-30 Color $35-45
Ref.- MET1 p. 185 (mug not listed)

358. **PANELLED HOBNAIL**
2 7/8" dia. x 2 1/4" ht.
Bryce Brothers was the maker of this mug in the 1880s. After 1891, it was made by the U. S. Glass Co. It was produced in clear, blue and possibly other colors.
Clear $10-15 Color $15-20
Ref.- GCF2 p. 202, WEPG p. s330 and 385

359. **FINDLAY HOBNAIL**
2 5/8" dia. x 2 3/8" ht.
This cup and saucer was probably made by the Columbia Glass Co. in the 1880s. It was made in clear, amber and blue.
Clear $35-45 Color $60-75
50% less without saucer
Ref.- None

360. **RAINDROP RINGS**
2 3/4" dia. x 2" ht.
This blue cup and saucer was probably made by the Columbia Glass Co. It has a handle similar to cups and saucers known to be made by this company. It is known only in blue, but was probably made in clear and amber also.
Blue $60-75
Ref.- None

361. **FINECUT IN CIRCLE**
2 3/4" dia. x 3 1/8" ht.
This mug was made in clear, canary and pale blue in the 1880s.
Clear $25-30 Color $40-50
Ref.- None

362. **POLKA DOT**
3" dia. x 3 1/2" ht.
This mug was made by the New Martinsville Glass Mfg. Co. about 1918. It is known in clear and cobalt.
Clear $15-20 Cobalt $30-35
Ref.- NM p.38 (advertisement)

363. **SAINT LOUIS**
1 3/8" dia. x 2" ht.
This mug was made by the Westmoreland Specialty Co. in the early 1900s. It is only known in clear and rose stain.
Clear $15-20 Stain $20-25
Ref.- TOY p. 139

361

364. **THUMBPRINT ON SPEARPOINT (TEARDROP & CRACKED ICE)**
2 7/8" dia. x 3 1/2" ht.
The Dalzell, Gilmore & Leighton Glass Co. was the manufacturer of this pattern about 1889, and the Cambridge Glass Co. also made it about 1903. It was made only in clear.
Clear $30-35
Ref.- CAM1, FIN p. 101, GCF2 p. 188,

365. **HOBNAIL WITH THUMBPRINT BASE (DOYLE'S NO. 150)**
smaller or 3 1/8" dia. x 3 3/4" ht.
Doyle & Co. was the maker of this mug in the 1880s. The U. S. Glass Co. made it after 1891. It was made in clear, green, blue and possibly other colors.
Both Sizes Clear $20-25
Both Sizes Green $35-40
Ref.- GCF2 p. 202, HOB1, KM7 p. 109 (advertisement)

366. **PRISCILLA (ALEXIS)**
3" dia. x 2 3/8" ht.
The Dalzell, Gilmore & Leighton Glass Co. was the manufacturer of this pattern about 1895. It is shown in an 1896 Montgomery Ward catalogue, where it is called "Crown Jewel." It was made in clear and is rare with ruby stained circles. The item of interest is a cup and saucer. There are over 50 different pieces in this pattern. The pattern has been reproduced in color.
Clear $40-45
Ref.- JLPG p. 422, MMPG p. 472

362

363

364

365

366

367

368

372

367. **MEDALLION SUNBURST**
2 5/8" dia. x 3 1/8" ht.
Bryce, Higbee & Co. manufactured this pattern about 1905. It was only produced in clear. Over 25 different pieces were made in this pattern.
Clear $25-30
Ref.- JLPG p. 364, WHPG p. 176

368. **SUNBURST IN OVAL (HEISEY'S NO. 343 1/2, DUNCAN & MILLER'S NO. 67)**
2 1/2" dia. x 2 7/8" ht.
The A. H. Heisey Glass Co. and Duncan & Miller Glass Co. made this pattern about the turn of the century. A tumbler with an applied handle is shown. It was made in clear and ruby stain.
Clear $35-40 Stain $50-60
Ref.- HC6 p. 79 (advertisement, but no mug), KM7 p. 50 & 140 (advertisement, but no mug)

369. **ATLAS (CRYSTAL BALL)**
p. 147 for pattern picture
This pattern was manufactured by Adams & Co. and Bryce Brothers in the 1880s, then by the U. S. Glass Co after 1891. This clear pattern has about 50 different items.
Clear $25-30
Ref.- JLPG p. 30

370. **ELECTRIC (U. S. GLASS' NO. 15038)**
p. 147 for pattern picture
The U. S. Glass Co. made this pattern in the 1890s. It is known only in clear.
Clear $25-30
Ref.- WEPG p. 361

371. **FROST CRYSTAL**
p. 147 for pattern picture
The Tarentum Glass Co. was the maker of this pattern about 1906. The item of interest is a custard cup. The pattern was produced only in clear and ruby stain.
Clear $15-20 Stain $30-35
Ref.- KM6 plate 51 (advertisement)

372. **THUMBPRINT & STAR BAND**
2 1/2" dia. x 3 1/4" ht.
The tartentum Glass Co. probably made this mug at the turn of the century. They are believed to be the only makers of green custard. Considered a souvenir, this mug was made in clear, yellow custard, green custard and ruby stain.
Color and Stain $30-35
Ref.- HCG1 p. 57 & 102

373. **HOBNAIL BAND**
not shown
This pattern was probably manufactured in the 1880s. The cup and saucer are known only in clear.
Clear $20-25
Ref.- MMPG p. 306

374. **ROSETTE (MAGIC)**
p. 147 for pattern picture
Bryce Brothers started producing this clear pattern in the late 1880s. After 1891, it was made by the U. S. Glass Co. There are over 35 different items in the pattern.
Clear $25-30
Ref.- JLPG p. 455, MET1 125, PG&B p. 86 (advertisement)

375

376

377

378

379

OVALS

375. **BROKEN COLUMN (U. S. GLASS' NO. 15021)**
(only the cup is shown)
This pattern was manufactured by the Columbia Glass Co. in the 1880s and by the U. S. Glass Co. after 1891. The cup and saucer are found in clear and a rare blue, Clear with ruby stained notches is scarce. Over 80 different pieces were made in this pattern.
Clear $45-55 Color and Stain $100-125 without saucer 50% less
Ref.- HCG1 p. 22 (advertisement), JLPG p. 82, MET1 p. 141, WHPG p. 50

376. **COTTAGE**
2 7/8" dia. x 2 3/4" ht. (only cup shown.)
Adams & Co. was the maker of this pattern about 1874. The U. S. Glass Co. reissued it after 1891. The items of interest here are a cup and saucer. It was made in clear, amber, blue and green. The larger handled items in the service have "hands" holding a bar at the handle. There are about 65 different items in the pattern.
Clear $40-50 Color $65-80 without saucer 50% less
Ref.- HC5 p. 63 (advertisement), JLPG p. 135, MET1 p. 153, MMPG p. 188

377. **DEWEY**
2 1/4" dia. x 3 1/2" ht.
The Indiana Tumbler & Goblet Co. of Greentown, Indiana, first made this mug about 1898. It was named in honor of Admiral Dewey because of his part in the Spanish-American War. It is also shown in a 1907-08 Indiana Glass Co. catalogue. There are many different items in this pattern. It was produced in clear, amber, blue, emerald green, olive green, canary, opaque white, nile green and chocolate.
Clear $40-50 Nile Green $200-250
Chocolate $350-450
Other Colors $55-85
Ref.- GRE p. 57, JLPG p. 176 GREE plate 277

378. **PICTURE FRAME**
3" dia. x 3 3/8" ht.
This mug was probably manufactured by Dithridge & Co. about 1879. It has the same shape and handle as Santa & Chimney and Little Red Riding Hood. It has a clear oval on each side. It was made in clear, amber and canary. The unusual molded surface treatment in this and other mugs is called "Crystalography". See Little Bo-Peep for description.
Clear $30-35 Color $40-50
Ref.- None

379. **SHUTTLE (HEART OF LOCH LAVEN)**
2 1/2" dia. x 3 1/4" ht.
This pattern, originally designated No. 29, was manufactured by the Indiana Tumbler & Goblet Co. about 1896. It is also shown in a 1907-08 Indiana Glass Co. catalogue. It was made in clear, amber, blue, green, and chocolate. There are more than 20 different items in the pattern.
Clear $20-25
Chocolate $100-150
Other Color $300-400
Ref.- GRE p. 50, GREE fig.38 and 277 (advertisement), JLPG p. 481, MET1 p. 211

380. **DAKOTA VARIANT**
2 3/8" dia. x 3 1/4" ht.
This mug was probably manufactured about 1900 and is known only in clear.
Clear $20-25
Ref.- None

381. **FRAMED JEWEL**
2 1/4" dia. x 3" ht.
The Canton Glass Co. was the maker of this mug about 1893. It was made in clear, with amethyst stain panels and with gold.
Clear $15-20 Stain $25-30
Ref.- HC7 p. 119

382. **COLUMBIA (U. S. GLASS' NO. 15082)**
2 3/4" dia. x 3 1/8" ht.
The U. S. Glass Co. was the manufacturer of this mug about 1903. It was made in clear, rose stain, and with gold.
Clear $15-20 Stain $30-35
Ref.- HC5 p. 152 (advertisement)

383. **CORDOVA**
2 5/8" dia. x 2 3/4" ht.
The pattern was manufactured by the O'Hara Glass Co. and by the U. S. Glass Co. after 1891. Produced in clear, green and ruby stain, the pattern has over 75 different items. John G. Lyon patented it on December 16, 1890.
Clear $15-20
Green and Stain $25-30
Ref.- JLPG p. 133

384. **WYCLIFF (SCROLL WITH STAR, CHALLINOR & TAYLOR'S NO. 310)**
3 3/8" dia. x 2 1/4" ht.
The Challinor, Taylor & Co. Ltd. made this pattern about 1890. In the early 1900s it was made by the U. S. Glass Co. The items shown are a cup and saucer. The pattern is known only in clear.
Clear $30-35
50% less without saucer
Ref.- HC5 p. 94 (advertisement), PAT p. 140 (cup and saucer not listed), WHPG p. 232

385. **WELLSBURG (NATIONAL GLASS NO. 681)**
2 5/8" dia. x 2 3/4" ht.
The National Glass Co. made this pattern about 1901. It was produced in clear and possibly ruby stain.
Clear $25-30
Ref.- A&C2 p.178, KM5 plate 5 (advertisement, but not not shown), MMPG p. 314 (mug not listed)

386
387
388
389
390
391
392
393
394
395
396
397

386. **PLEATED SKIRT WITH OVALS**
2" dia. x 3 1/4" ht.
This mug was probably made after 1900. It is similar to Pleated Skirt, except it has a row of ovals above the pleating. It is known in clear, amber and blue.
Clear $25-30 Color $30-35
Ref.- None

387. **MICHIGAN (BULGING LOOPS, U. S. GLASS NO. 15077)**
lemonade: 2 3/4" dia. x 4" ht. or cup
The U. S. Glass Co. made this pattern. It was shown in a 1902 Sear catalogue as Michigan. The item shown is a lemonade. It was produced in clear, with rose stain, with yellow stain, with blue stain and is rare with ruby stain. About 85 different pieces are available in the pattern.
Cup Clear $15-20 Cup Stain and Lemonade Clear $25-30 Lemonade Stain $50-60
Ref.- HC5 p. 152 (advertisement), JLPG p. 368, MET1 p. 195, MMPG p. 438

388. **LOUSIANA (U. S. GLASS NO. 15053)**
3" dia. x 3 5/8" ht.
Bryce Brothers was the maker of this pattern in the 1880s. After 1891, it was made by the U. S. Glass Co. It was produced in clear and frosted (acid etched). The pattern has about 45 different items.
Clear $25-30 Frosted $35-40
Ref.- JLPG p. 344, MMPG p. 238

389. **GEORGIA (PEACOCK FEATHER, U. S. GLASS' NO. 15076)**
2 1/4" dia. x 3 3/8" ht.
The U. S. Glass Co. manufactured this pattern about 1905. The mug is shown in a 1914 Federal Glass Co. Packer's Catalogue. The pattern was produced in clear and is rare in amber and blue. The pattern has about 40 different items.
Clear $35-40
Ref.- HGC5 p. 39 (advertisement), JLPG p. 243, MMPG p. 58

390. **LOOP WITH DEWDROP (U. S. GLASS NO. 15028)**
2 1/2" dia. x 2 7/8" ht.
The U. S. Glass Co. made this pattern about 1892. Clear is the only way it was made. The pattern has about 40 different items.
Clear $20-25
Ref.- LEE p. 256, MMPG p. 312

391. **STIPPLED ARROW**
1 3/8" dia. x 1 3/4" ht.
This mug is shown in a 1914 Federal Glass Co. Packer's Catalogue. It was made in clear and turquoise.
Clear $15-20 Turquoise $25-30
Ref.- GCF1 p. 90, HGC5 p. 40 (advertisement), TOY p. 138

392. **LONG OPTIC (TYCOON)**
custard cup or mug: smaller or 3" dia. x 3 1/4" ht.
The Columbia Glass Co. was the maker of this pattern about 1890. It is known only in clear. The mug was sold with and without a cover. A cover indicates that a retailer sold the mug with another product inside, such as jelly or mustard.
All Mugs Clear $20-25 Cup $10-15
Ref.- FIN p. 42 and 38 (advertisement), FINP p. 56, HOB1, PG&B p. 126 (advertisement), TOY p. 157

393. **PICKET & THUMBPRINT**
1 3/4" dia. x 2 3/8" ht.
This mug has an "H" on the bottom. It was probably made after 1900 since few trademarks were used before that date. I am unaware of whose trademark this is. The picket design is the same as Riverside Glass Co.'s No. 364 shown in RIV p. 49 (advertisement). It is known only in clear.
Clear $25-30
Ref.- None

394. **CUT LOG (ETHOL)**
2 5/8" dia. x 3 1/4" ht.
Bryce, Higbee & Co. and the Westmoreland Specialty Glass Co. were the manufacturers of this pattern about 1889. It was produced in clear and rare frosted. The pattern has over 60 different items.
Clear $20-25 Frosted $35-45
Ref.- JLPG p. 147, KM8 p.153 & 155 (advertisement - mug not shown), MET1 p. 143, MMPG p. 418

395. **ARCHED OVALS VARIANT**
2 1/8" dia. x 2 3/4" ht.
This mug was probably made in the 1890s. It is known only in clear.
Clear $15-20
Ref.- None

396. **KANSAS (JEWEL W/ DEWDROP, U. S. GLASS' NO. 15072)**
2 1/8" dia. x 3 3/8" ht. or 2 7/8" dia. x 3 1/2" ht.
The U. S. Glass Co. made this pattern about 1901. The table service has about 55 items. The small mug was made by the D. C. Jenkins Glass Co. about 1906. It was shown in a 1914 Federal Glass Co. Packer's Catalogue. The mug was produced in clear, with stained jewels on the large size, ruby stained top on the small size and with gold. The small mug has been reproduced in amber, blue and canary.
Sm. Clear $20-25 Lg. Clear $40-45 Sm. Stain $30-35
Ref.- A&C2 p.235 (advertisement), GREE fig.282, HGC5 p. 39 (advertisement), JJ p. 79 (advertisement) JLPG p. 307, MET2 p. 107, WHPG p. 154

397. **HAND (PENNSYLVANIA)**
3 1/8" dia. x 3 1/2" ht.
The O'Hara Glass Co. made this pattern in the 1880s. This rare mug is a tumbler with an applied handle. The finial on the covered pieces is a hand holding a bar. Made only in clear, the pattern has about 30 different items.
Clear $60-75
Ref.- JLPG p. 260

396

399

400

401

393. **RIBBON CANDY (U. S. GLASS' NO. 15010)**
p. 147 for pattern picture
This pattern was manufactured by the Bryce Brothers in the 1880s. After 1891, it was made by the U. S. Glass Co. There are over 75 different items in the pattern, which was made in clear with odd items in green.
Clear $20-25
Ref.- WHPG p. 438

394. **DAKOTA (BABY THUMBPRINT)**
2 3/4" dia. x 3 1/2" ht.
Ripley & Co. was the maker of this pattern in the 1880s and was continued by the U. S. Glass Co. after 1891. This is a tumbler with an applied handle. The pattern was made in clear, etched, ruby stain, and is rare in cobalt. The pattern has about 60 different items. The mug is often souvenired.
Clear $35-40 Stain $60-70
Ref.- JLPG p. 165, MET1 p. 145

395. **ARCHED OVALS (U. S. GLASS' NO. 15091)**
2" dia. x 2 1/2" ht. or 2 5/8" dia. x 2 7/8" ht. or 3" dia. x 3 1/4" ht.
This pattern was manufactured by Ripley & Co. in the 1880s and was continued by the U. S. Glass Co. after 1891. It was produced in clear, green, rose stain and ruby stain. It was a popular souvenired item.
All Sizes Clear $20-25 All Sizes Green and Stain $30-40
Ref.- RS plate 9

396. **BORDERED ELLIPSE**
2 3/8" dia. x 2 7/8" ht.
This pattern was manufactured by McKee Glass Co. and the Lancaster Glass Co. about 1896. It was produced in clear, blue, and ruby stain.
Clear $20-25 Blue and Stain $35-40
Ref.- MMPG p. 206, RS plate 13, HC7 p. 45

402

403

404

DIAMONDS

402. **AURORA (DIAMOND HORSESHOE)**
The Brilliant Glass Works and the Greensburg Glass Co. manufactured this pattern in the late 1880s. It was produced in clear, etched and ruby stained. There are about 35 different items in this pattern.
Clear $35-45 Stain $55-65
Ref.- KM8 p. 160 (advertisement), JLPG p. 32, MET1 p. 195

403. **DIAMOND FLUTE (JEANNETTE, FLAMBOYANT)**
3" dia. x 1 7/8" ht.
McKee & Brother made this pattern. The cup and saucer are shown in an 1886 catalogue. The cup is marked McKEE & BROS JEANNETTE PA. It was made only in clear.
Clear $20-25 50% less without saucer
Ref.- HC6 p. 91 (advertisement)

404. **GRATED DIAMOND & SUNBURST (DUNCAN'S NO. 20)**
3" dia. x 3 3/4" ht.
George Duncan's Sons made this pattern about 1890. The mug is a water tumbler with an applied twisted reed handle. The pattern was made only in clear.
Clear $25-30
Ref.- KM7 p. 122 (advertisement, mug not shown)

405. **GALLOWAY (MIRROR, U. S. GLASS' NO. 15086)**
small or 3" dia. x 4" ht.
The U. S. Glass Co. was the maker of this pattern in the early 1900s. It was produced in clear, rose stain, ruby stain and with gold. The larger size mug is a lemonade. The table service has about 60 items.
Both Sizes Clear $30-35
Both Sizes Stain $50-65
Ref.- HC5 p. 154 (advertisement), JLPG p. 239, WHPG p. 122

406. **DEEP STAR**
2 1/2" dia. x 3 1/4" ht.
The Model Flint Glass Co. was the maker of this mug about 1889. It is known only in clear.
Clear $20-25
Ref.- FIN p. 128, FINP p. 88

407. **PARAGON (HEAVY PANELLED FINECUT)**
3 1/4" dia. x 3 3/4" ht.
A tumbler with applied handle is shown. Adams & Co. was the maker of this clear pattern in the 1880s. The U. S. Glass Co. took over production after 1891. A 4 piece caster set is the only other item known.
Clear $25-30
Ref.- HC7 p. 168 (mug not listed)

408. **DIAMOND RIDGE (DUNCAN & MILLER'S NO. 48)**
2 7/8" dia. x 3 1/4" ht. or
2 5/8" dia. x 3 1/2" ht. (footed)
This mug was manufactured by the Duncan & Miller Glass Co. about 1901. It was made in clear, ruby stain and with gold.
Clear & with Gold $20-25
Stain with Gold $35-40
Ref.- HC7 p. 105 (mug not listed)

409. **BANDED STALKS**
2 1/2" dia. x 2 3/4" ht.
This mug was manufactured after 1900. It was made in clear only.
Clear $20-25
Ref.- GCF1 p. 83, TOY p. 154

410. **DIAMOND BAND (CLEAR DIAMOND)**
2 3/8" dia. x 3 3/8" ht.
This mug was probably manufactured in the 1890s. It is known only in clear.
Clear $15-20
Ref.- GCF1 p. 85

411. **DIAMOND BAND VARIANT**
1 1/2" dia. x 2 1/8" ht.
This mug was probably made in the 1880s. It is known only in clear.
Clear $15-20
Ref.- TOY p. 139

412. **PRISM ARC (X-LOG)**
2 1/2" dia. x 2 3/4" ht. or
2 7/8" dia. x 3 1/8" ht.
The Co-operative Flint Glass Co. probably made this pattern about 1893. The pattern was produced in clear, ruby stain and opaque white.
Clear $25-30
Ref.- MMPG p. 174, WHPG p. 285

413. **PINEAPPLE & FAN (U. S. GLASS NO. 15041)**
2 3/8" dia. x 2 3/8" ht.
Adams & Co. made this pattern in the 1880s. The U. S. Glass Co. produced it after 1891. It was produced in clear only. The pattern contains more than 30 different items.
Clear $15-20
Ref.- HC5 p. 152 (advertisement), WHPG p. 205

405

406

407

408

409

410

411

412

414. **ROYAL CRYSTAL (TARENTUM'S ATLANTA)**
2 3/4" dia. x 2 5/8" ht.
This pattern was manufactured by the Tarentum Glass Co. about 1894. It was made in clear and ruby stain. This item is a custard cup.
Clear $10-15 Stain $15-20
Ref.- HC7 p. 69 (advertisement, cup not listed)

415. **DIAMOND & RECTANGLE PANELS**
3" dia. x 3 3/4" ht.
This pattern was made in amber, blue canary and apple green about 1880.
Color $30-35
Ref.- None

416. **PETTICOAT (NATIONAL)**
2 5/8" dia. x 2 7/8" ht.
The Riverside Glass Co. was the maker of this scarce pattern about 1899. It was made in clear, canary and both with gold. There is a 4 piece table set, a water set, a berry set, a celery, a cruet, a syrup, a mustard and 3 sizes of hat sizes.
Clear $40-45 Canary $70-90
Ref.- HC1 p. 35, HCO p. 118 (mug not listed), RIV p. 190 and 191

412

414

415

416

417. **O'HARA DIAMOND (SAWTOOTH & STAR, U. S. GLASS' NO. 15001)**
p. 147 for pattern picture
Ohara Glass Co. made this pattern in the 1880s. After 1891, it was manufactured by the U. Glass Co. It was produced only in clear.
Mug $25-30 Cup and Suacer $40-50 without saucer 50% less
Ref.- KM8 p. 112 (advertisement), PG&B p. 273 (advertisement)

418. **DIAMOND QUILTED**
p. 147 for pattern picture
The manufacture of this pattern probably occurred in the 1880s. The mug was made in amber and blue. About 25 different items were made in both colors.
Color $25-35
Ref.- JLPG p. 181

419. **FINECUT & BLOCK**
p. 147 for pattern picture
King, Son & Co., and the Model Flint Glass Co. were the makers of this pattern about 1890. The pattern has about 70 different items; most are available in these colors: clear, amber, blue, canary, and with painted color blocks in amber, blue and pink.
Clear $20-25
Stain and Color $35-40
Ref.- JLPG p. 211

420. **JACOB'S LADDER (MALTESE)**
Bryce, Walker & Co. was the maker of this pattern about 1876. The mug is a tumbler with an applied handle. The pattern has been produced in clear, amber, blue and amethyst. Items in color are rare. The dolphin footed compote and the mug are extremely rare. Over 60 different pieces were made in this pattern. The pattern was reproduced starting in 1988 (not the mug). This is primarily is bright red and bright green.
Clear $150-175
Ref.- HC5 p. 85 (advertisement), JLPG p. 298, LEE p. 358, MET1 p. 141

420

421. **POINTED JEWEL (U. S. GLASS' NO. 15006)**
The Columbia Glass Co. was the maker of this pattern in the late 1880s. After 1891, it was made by the U. S. Glass Co. The items of interest are a cup and saucer. The pattern was produced in clear and is scarce in opaque white.
Clear $45-55
without saucer 50% less
Ref.- HC5 p. 131 (advertisement), KM6 plate 1 (advertisement), PG&B p. 127 (advertisement), WHPG p. 208

421

422. **WESTMORELAND (U. S. GLASS' NO. 15011)**
p. 147 for pattern picture
This pattern was patented by Thomas W. Mellor in 1889 and assigned to Gillinder & Sons. After 1891, it was made by the U. S. Glass Co. The item shown is a punch cup. The pattern was only produced in clear. Over 75 different pieces were made in the pattern.
Clear $10-15
Ref.- LEEV p. 149, WHPG p. 278

423. **NOVA SCOTIA DIAMOND**
2 1/8" dia. x 3 1/2" ht.
The Nova Scotia Glass Co. and the Burlington Glass Works made this pattern in the 1880s. It was made only in clear.
Clear $20-25
Ref.- NOVA p. 27, 39 and 40 (mug not listed)

423

424. **VICTORIA, PIONEER'S**
p. 147 for pattern picture
This pattern was decorated by the Pioneer Glass Co, Ltd. in the early 1900s. The actual manufacturer is unknown. The item of interest is called a lemonade, but it is whatwould normally be called a custard. It was produced in clear and ruby stain.
Clear $10-15 Stain $15-20
Ref.- KM8 p. 176 (advertisement)

425

426

427

428

429

430

425. **DIAMOND POINT BAND**
2 1/2" dia. x 3 1/4" ht.
The U. S. Glass Co. made this mug about 1896. It was made in clear, green, ruby stain and yellow-green. Some items are souvenired. A goblet and a wine are also known.
Clear $20-25
Stain and Green $30-40
Ref.- HC7 p. 198 (mug not listed)

426. **PAVONIA (PINEAPPLE STEM)**
3" dia. x 3 3/4" ht.
Ripley & Co. manufactured this pattern in the 1880s. After 1891, the U. S. Glass Co. took over production. This is a water tumbler with an applied handle. It was made in clear and ruby stain. The ruby stained pieces were often etched souvenirs. There are about 60 different items in the pattern.
Clear $35-40 Stain $50-60
Ref.- JLPG p. 401, HC7 p. 169

427. **TRIPLE TRIANGLE**
2 3/8" dia. x 3" ht.
Doyle & Co. made this pattern in the 1880s. After 1891, it was made by the U. S. Glass Co. It was produced in clear and ruby stain. There are about 25 different items in the pattern.
Clear $30-35 Stain $40-45
Ref.- JLPG p. 527, KM8 p. 105 (advertisement), MET1 p. 221, MMPG p. 174

428. **DIAMOND WITH CIRCLE**
2 3/4" dia. x 3" ht.
This pattern was probably made in the 1880s. It was produced in clear, amber, blue, and apple green. It is probably a companion piece to Upright Rabbit and Wolf, because the twig handle design is very similar.
Clear $30-35 Color $45-55
Ref.- GCF1 p. 83

429. **P OINTED ARCHES**
2 5/8" dia. x 3 1/4" ht.
This ruby stained mug was probably made about 1910.
Stain $30-35
Ref.- PP1 p. 73

430. **CROSS HATCHING**
1 7/8" dia. x 2" ht.
This mug was made by Bryce Brothers in the 1880s. It was produced in clear, amber and blue.
Clear $20-25 Color $35-45
Ref.- PG&B p. 90 (advertisement), TOY p. 141

431. **ART (TEARDROPS & DIAMOND BLOCK)**
p. 147 for pattern picture
This pattern was manufactured by Adams & Co. in the 1880s and by the U.S. Glass Co. after 1891. This is probably a tumbler with an applied handle. It was made in clear and ruby stained. The pattern has about 75 different pieces.
Clear $40-50 Stain $60-75
Ref.- JLPG p. 23, WHPG p. 21

432. **DIAMONDS**
1 7/8" dia. x 2 3/4" ht. not shown
This cup and saucer was probably made in the 1880s. They were produced in clear, opaque blue and possibly other colors.
Clear $40-50 Opaque Blue $80-100 without saucer 50% less
Ref.- GCF1 p. 51, TOY p. 133

FACETS

433. **MASSACHUSETTS (U. S. GLASS' NO. 15054)**
mug: 2 7/8" dia. x 3 1/4" ht. or lemonade: 2 1/2" dia. x 4 1/4" ht.
This pattern was manufactured by the U. S. Glass Co. about 1898. The mug can be found with advertising. It reads, "LANDSBURGH & BRO / DRY GOODS ONLY / WASHINGTON/D.C." The pattern was produced in clear, ruby stain, green and cobalt, but it is rare in any color. There are about 100 different pieces in this pattern. A complete lamp is difficult to find. The butter has been reproduced in color.
Clear mug $25-30 Clear Lemonade $40-50 add 100% for advertising
Ref.- JLPG p. 362, MMPG p. 232

434. **SEDAN (PANELLED STAR & BUTTON)**
2 1/8" dia. x 2 7/8" ht.
This pattern was probably made about the 1900. There are about 20 different pieces in the pattern, which was produced in clear and a rare purple slag.
Large Clear $15-20
Ref.- JLPG p. 473

435. **SEDAN VARIANT**
1 3/4" dia. x 2 1/4" ht.
This mug was probably manufactured in the 1880s. It is known in cobalt blue and opalescent. The shape and size of this mug is very similar to Panelled Cane. It is quite possible that they were made at the same factory.
Color $30-35
Ref.- None

436. **TORPEDO (PIGMY)**
2 7/8" dia. x 2 1/2" ht.
The Thompson Glass Co. made this pattern about 1890. It is shown in an 1894 Montgomery Wards Catalogue. However, the factory stopped production in 1892. It was made in clear and ruby stain. The cup and saucer is only known in clear.
Clear $55-65 50% less without saucer
Ref.- JLPG p. 523

433

434

435

436

437. **CANE INSERT**
not shown
This pattern was made by the Tarentum Glass Co. about 1900. It was produced in clear, green, custard, green custard and with gold. Over 20 different pieces were made in this pattern.
Clear $15-20
Color $30-35
Ref.- WHPG p. 60

438. **BUCKLE & STAR (ORIENT)**
This pattern was made by Bryce, Walker & Co. about 1880 and was reissued by the U. S. Glass Co. after 1891. It may have been made by the Burlington Glass Works. It was produced only in clear. The pattern has about 30 different items.
Clear $55-65
Ref.- HC5 p. 85 (advertisement), JLPG p. 85

438

439. **KALONYAL (HEISEY'S NO. 1776)**
p. 147 for pattern picture
A. H. Heisey & Co. was the maker of this pattern between 1904 and 1908. The items of interest here are a custard cup and a mug. It was made in clear, ruby stain and with gold.
Clear $15-20 Stain $30-35
Ref.- HSY p. 30, KM7 p. 142 (advertisement), MMPG p. 456

440

441

442

443

444

445

440. **FINECUT & PANEL**
3 1/8" dia. x 4" ht.
This pattern was made by Bryce Brothers and the Richards & Hartley Glass Co. in the late 1880s. The U. S. Glass Co. took over production in 1891. The item shown is a water tumbler with an applied handle. The pattern was made in clear, amber, blue and canary.
Clear $35-40 Color $50-70
Ref.- JLPG p. 212 (mug not listed)

441. **RAINBOW**
3" dia. x 2 3/8" ht.
McKee Brothers & Co. shows this "lemonade cup" in a 1901 catalogue. It was also illustrated in a 1900 Sears catalogue. The pattern was still being offered in 1927. The pattern was made in clear and ruby stain. Over 40 different pieces were made in this pattern.
Clear $10-15 Stain $20-25
Ref.- HC6 p. 67 (advertisement), HC7 p. 183 (mug not listed)

442. **AUSTRIAN (No. 200 / FINECUT MEDALLION)**
2 3/4" dia. x 3 1/8" ht.
The Indiana Tumbler & Goblet Co. was the maker of this pattern about 1897. It was probably continued by the National Glass Co. after 1899. The pattern is also shown in a 1907-08 Indiana Glass Co. catalogue. The pattern has about 40 different items. It was produced in clear, amber, a rare amethyst, blue-green and canary.
Clear $40-45 Color $200-300
Ref.- GRE p. 54, GREE fig.48 and 277 (advertisement), JLPG p. 33

443. **LACY DAISY (U. S. GLASS' NO. 9525)**
3" dia. x 2 1/2" ht.
This mug was made by the U. S. Glass Co. about 1918. It was made in clear and in limited color.
Clear $15-20
Ref.- HC5 p. 162 (advertisement)

444. **DAISY & BUTTON WITH OVAL MEDALLION (PEARL)**
2 1/2" dia. x 2 5/8" ht.
The Co-Operative Flint Glass Co. was the maker of this pattern in the 1880s. It is known only in clear.
Clear $25-30
Ref.- HC7 p. 242 (advertisement, no mug)

445. **LACY DAISY, NEW MARTINSVILLE'S**
2 3/8" dia. x 2 3/8" ht.
The base of the mustard is shown. The J. B. Higbee Higbee Glass Co. made this piece about 1908. After 1919, it was made by the New Martinsville Glass Manufacturing Co. It was only produced in clear.
Clear $20-25 50% more with cover
Ref.- MET1 p. 64, TOY p. 137, WHPG p. 157

446

447

448

449

450

451

446. **BUTTON ARCHES**
mug: 2 3/8" dia. x 2 3/4" ht. or 2 3/8" dia. x 3 1/4" ht. or cup: 2 3/4" dia. x 2 1/8" ht.
This pattern was made by George Duncan's Sons Co. about 1897 and by Duncan & Miller Glass Co. starting about 1900. It was made in clear, ruby stain, ruby stain with frosted band, alabaster and opaque white. Opaque white was called "Koral". There are about 30 different items in the pattern.
Both Sizes Mug Clear $20-25 Both Sizes Mug Color and Stain $30-35
Cup Clear $10-15
Cup Color and Stain $15-20
Ref.- HC6 p. 80 (advertisement), HC7 p. 38, JLPG p. 95, KM6 plate 9 (advertisement), MMPG p. 202, WHPG p. 55

447. **DAISY & BUTTON WITH "V" ORNAMENT (VAN DYKE)**
2 5/8" ht., 2 3/8" dia. x 2 7/8" ht. or 2 5/8" dia. x 3 1/8" ht. or 3" dia. x 3 3/8" ht.
This pattern was manufactured by the A. J. Beatty Co. in the 1880s and continued by the U. S. Glass Co. after 1891. It was made in clear, amber, blue and canary. The pattern has about 40 different items in all colors.
All Sizes Clear $15-20 All Sizes Color $25-35
Ref.- GCF1 p. 89, HC5 p. 112 (advertisement), JLPG p. 162, LEE p. 592, PG&B p. 57 (advertisement), TOY p. 140, WEPG p. 243

448. **BOX IN BOX**
2 1/4" dia. x 2 3/4" ht.
The Riverside Glass Co. manufactured this pattern about 1900. It was made in clear, ruby stain and green.
Clear $20-25
Green and Stain $35-40
Ref.- HC7 p. 80, RIV p. 83

449. **CAMBRIDGE'S NO. 2658**
2 3/4" dia. x 2 7/8" ht.
The Cambridge Glass Co. was the maker of this mug about 1910. Cambridge's trademark, "Nearcut" is pressed in the base. It was made in clear, clear with enamel, marigold carnival and ruby stain, often souvenir etched.
Clear $20-25 Marigold $150-175
Stain $30-35
Ref.- CAM2 p. 84

450. **BLOCK (RED BLOCK, AMBER BLOCK, CLEAR BLOCK)**
2 1/2" dia. x 3" ht.
The makers of this pattern were Bryce Brothers, the Central Glass Co., Doyle & Co., the Fostoria Glass Co., George Duncan & Sons, The Model Flint Glass Works and the U. S. Glass Co. between 1885 and 1907. It was made in clear, ruby stain, amber stain and with gold. The pattern has about 40 different items.
Clear $20-25 Ruby Stain $30-35
Amber Stain $40-45
Ref.- JLPG p. 432, KM7 p. 112 (advertisement), LEE p. 543, MET1 p. 165, PG&B p. 139 (advertisement)

451. **SUNKEN HONEYCOMB (CORONA)**
2 3/4" dia. x 2 7/8" ht.
This pattern was manufactured by the Greensburg Glass Co. in the 1890s. From 1899 to 1903 it was made by the National Glass Co. From 1903 until the 1920s, it was made by the McKee Glass Co. It was produced in clear and ruby stain. Many of the ruby stained and blue-green pieces were souvenired. Over 25 different items were made in the pattern.
Clear $60-70 Stain and Blue-Green $90-110 without saucer 50% less
Ref.- HC7 p. 42 (advertisement), MK p. 121 (advertisement)

452

453

454

455

456

457

452. **DAISY & BUTTON BOTTOM**
smaller or 2 3/4" dia. x 3 5/8" ht. or lgr.
This blue mug was made in the 1880s and is known only as a souvenir. It was probably made in clear and other colors.
All Sizes Blue $40-50
Ref.- HC5 p. 162 (advertisement)

453. **DAISY & BUTTON WITH CROSSBAR**
2 5/8" dia. x 2 7/8" ht. or 3" dia. x 3 3/8" ht.
The Burlington Glass Works and the Richards & Hartley Glass Co. manufactured this pattern in the 1880s. The U. S. Glass Co. continued production after 1891. It was made clear, dark amber, light amber, blue and canary. The pattern has about 45 different items.
Both Sizes Clear $10-15 Both Sizes Color $20-30
Ref.- HC5 p. 112 (advertisement), JLPG p. 157, MMPG p. 176, TAR p. 200

454. **FACETED (DOYLE'S NO. 500)**
2" dia. x 2" ht. or 2 1/4" dia. x 2 3/8" ht.
This children's pattern was manufactured by Doyle & Co. in the 1880s and by the U. S. Glass Co.after 1891. It was produced in clear, amber, blue and canary. The other pieces made were a 4 piece table set (sugar, creamer, spooner and covered butter).
Both Sizes Clear $20-25 Both Sizes Color $35-40
Ref.- GCF1 p. 59, PG&B p. 139 (advertisement)

455. **PANELLED CANE (JEWEL)**
1 3/4" dia. x 2 1/4" ht. or
2 3/8" dia. x 2 3/4" ht. or
3 1/8" dia. x 3 1/4" ht.
This pattern has been attributed to the Portland Glass Co. about 1870, however, the colors are more typical of the 1880s or later. Portland stopped production in 1873. It was made in clear, amber, blue, canary and apple green.
All Sizes in Clear $20-30
All Sizes in Color $35-55
Ref.- GCF1 p. 88, TOY p. 140

456. **SCALLOPED DAISY & BUTTON (GILLINDER'S NO. 413)**
2 5/8" dia. x 3 1/8" ht.
Gillinder & Sons made this mug in the 1880s. It is known in clear, blue, and canary.
Clear $20-25 Color $40-50
Ref.- HOB1, TOY p. 157

457. **DIAMOND WITH PEG**
2 1/4" dia. x 2 3/8" ht. or 3" dia. x 3 1/8" ht.
The McKee Glass Co. was the maker of this pattern starting about 1894. After 1916, the same molds were used by the Jefferson Glass Co. Many items are marked "Krys-tol" which is a McKee trademark. It was made in ruby stain and custard. These were popular souvenir items. Only the Jefferson Glass Co. made custard.
Both Sizes Clear $20-25 Both Sizes Custard and Stain $30-40
Ref.- HC4 p. 49

ORNATE

458. **BALDER (PENNSYLVANIA, U. S. GLASS' NO. 15048)**
3 1/8" dia. x 2 7/8" ht.
The U. S. Glass Co. made this pattern about 1900. A custard is shown. It was produced in clear, green and ruby stain. There are over 65 different items in the pattern.
Clear $10-15
Green and Stain $20-25
Ref.- JLPG p. 403

459. **WEBB (PADEN CITY'S NO. 203)**
2 7/8" dia. x 3 1/8" ht.
The J. B. Higbee Glass Co. was the maker of this pattern about 1910. After 1918, it was manufactured by The Paden City Glass Manufacturing Co. The mug and several of the other items have the Higbee trademark, a bee with "H I G" on the wings and body. This pattern was made only in clear. This pattern has often been mistaken for Scalloped Daisy & Fans, which was made in color. See GOBI p. 311 and "Goblets II" plate 35 by S. T. Millard. There are over 35 different pieces in the pattern.
Clear $25-30
Ref.- HC6 p. 93 (advertisement), PC p. 39 (advertisement)

460. **OMNIBUS (HOBSTAR, U. S. GLASS' NO. 15124)**
3 1/8" dia. x 2 1/2" ht.
The U. S. Glass Co. made this pattern about 1915. A punch cup or a custard is shown. It was only produced in clear.
Clear $10-15
Ref.- WHPG p. 137

461. **CANE HORSESHOE (U. S. GLASS' NO. 15118)**
2 5/8" dia. x 3 1/2" ht.
This pattern was manufactured by the U. S. Glass Co. about 1909. It was made in clear, with gold and is rare in amber stain. The pattern has about 35 different pieces.
Clear $20-25 Stain $50-60
Ref.- JLPG p. 107

462. **DAISY IN DIAMOND**
1 7/8" dia. x 2 1/2" ht.
The O'Hara Glass Co. was the maker of this pattern in the 1880s and after 1891 the U. S. Glass Co. made it. The colors that it was produced in are clear, amber and blue. There are very few items in the pattern.
Clear $20-25 Color $35-40
Ref.- MMPG p. 236, WHPG p. 87

463. **ADMIRAL (RIBBED ELLIPSE)**
3" dia. x 3 1/8" ht.
This pattern was manufactured by Bryce, Higbee & Co. about 1899. It was only produced in clear. Over 25 different pieces were made in this pattern.
Clear $25-30
Ref.- HCP1 p. 7 (advertisement), HCP3 p. 7 (advertisement), MMPG p. 88, WHPG p. 12

464. **DUNCAN'S NO. 40**
2 1/4" dia. x 2 7/8" ht.
This pattern was made by George Duncan's Sons & Co. about 1898 and later by the Duncan & Miller Glass Co. It was produced in clear. Over 40 different pieces were manufactured in this pattern.
Clear $20-25
Ref.- MMPG p. 210 (mug not listed)

465. **LADDERS (TARTENTUM'S NO. 292)**
2 3/4" dia. x 2" ht.
The Tarentum Glass Co. made this cup and saucer about 1901. It was produced in clear and with gold.
Clear $25-30
50% less without saucer
Ref.- TAR p.331 (mug not listed)

466. **ARROWHEAD IN OVALS (MADORA)**
The J. B. Higbee Glass Co. was the maker of this pattern about 1910. After 1918, it was made by the Jefferson Glass Co. The mug is made in clear and ruby stain. Some stained pieces are souvenir. The pattern has over 75 different pieces.
Clear $25-30 Stain $50-60
Ref.- HC7 p. 147, HCG2 p. 25 (advertisement)

467. **REXFORD (ALPHA)**
custard cup: 3 1/8" dia. x 2 5/8" ht. or mug: 2 7/8" dia. x 3 3/8" ht.
This pattern was manufactured by the J. B. Higbee Glass Co. about 1910. It is shown in a Butler Brothers catalogue from 1910 and is called Cut Jewel. Several items have the Higbee trademark, a bee with a "H, I & G" on the wings and body. After 1918, it was manufactured by the New Martinsville Glass Manufacturing Co. It was made in clear and is rare in ruby stain. There are over 75 different items in the pattern.
Mug Clear $25-30 Cup Clear $10-15
Ref.- HC6 p. 96 (advertisement, but no mug), NM p. 24 (advertisement, but no mug), WEPG p. 363 (mug not listed)

468. **RUSTIC**
Gillinder & Sons made this mug about 1889. It is known only in clear.
Clear $20-25
Ref.- HOB1, PG&B p. 164 (advertisement), TOY p. 157

469. **YOKED DAISY**
3 1/4" dia. x 4 1/8" ht.
This footed mug was probably made about 1915. It is known only in clear.
Clear $20-25
Ref.- GOBII p. 67 (mug not listed)

458

459

460

461

462

463

464

465

466

467

468

469

470

471

472

473

474

475

470. **BRILLIANT, RIVERSIDE'S**
2 3/8" dia. x 3 1/2" ht.
The Riverside Glass Co. made this pattern about 1895. The mug was made in clear, ruby stain and amber stain. The mug becomes a mustard when a slotted cover is added.
Clear $35-45 Stain $70-90 add 50% with cover
Ref.- JLPG p. 77 (mug not listed), RIV p. 93 (advertisement, but no mug)

471. **CROSSED CORDS & PRISMS**
2" dia. x 1 7/8" ht. or 3 1/8" dia. x 3" ht.
Atterbury & Co. was probably the manufacturer of these mugs about 1880. Atterbury is the only company we know of that made this range of colors. The mugs were produced in clear, pink alabaster, opaque white, opaque black, amber and probably other colors.
Both Sizes Clear $15-20 Both Sizes Color $25-35
Ref.- GCD1, TOY p. 140

472. **DOYLE'S SHELL (CUBE & FAN)**
2 3/8" dia. x 3" ht.
This mug was manufactured by Doyle & Co. in the 1880s. The U. S. Glass Co. made it after 1891. It was made in clear, amber, ruby stain and possibly blue.
Clear $20-25 Stain $35-40
Ref.- LEEV p. 159, PG&B p. 139, TOY p. 156

473. **PINEAPPLE & FAN, HEISEY'S (HEISEY'S NO. 1255)**
2 5/8" dia. x 3 1/4" ht.
The A. H. Heisey Glass Co. made this pattern from 1897 to 1907. It was made in clear, green, with gold and is scarce in ruby stain. There are about 30 different items in the pattern.
Clear $25-30
Green and Stain $45-55
Ref.- HSY p. 45, JLPG p. 406, KM7 p. 136 (advertisement), MMPG p. 168

474. **SLINKY BAND**
3 1/8" dia. x 5" ht.
This stein was probably made about 1890. It was only produced in opaque white.
Opaque White $50-60
Ref.- None

475. **MISSOURI (PALM & SCROLL, U. S. GLASS' NO. 15058)**
3" dia. x 3 1/2" ht.
The U. S. Glass Co. made this pattern about 1898. It was produced in clear and green. It is rare in blue, amethyst and canary. Over 35 different pieces were made in this pattern.
Clear $30-40 Green $40-50 Other Colors $60-75
Ref.- JLPG p. 373, A&C2 p.234 (advertisement)

476

477

478

479

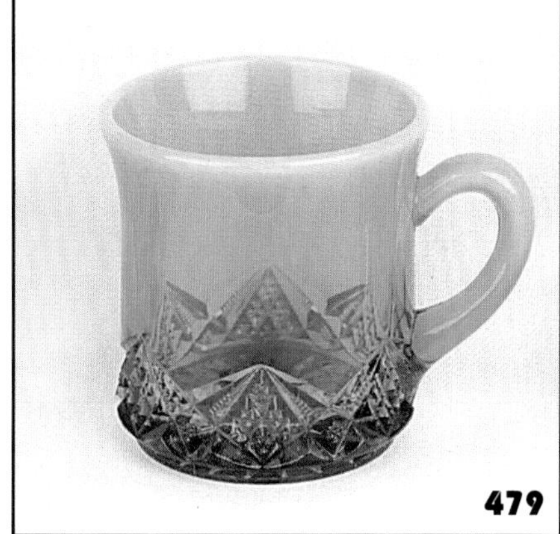
479

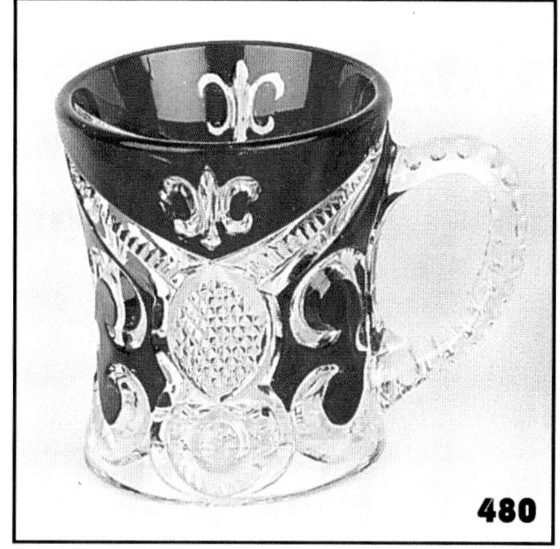
480

476. **BUCKINGHAM (CROSBY, U. S. GLASS' NO. 15106)**
3" dia. x 3 1/2" ht.
The U. S. Glass Co. was the maker of this pattern about 1907. It was made in clear, rose stain and with colored panels with gold. Most mugs have a star on the bottom, however, there is a variation that has a bottom that reads, "B. A. OF U. S. GLASS CO. / MERCHANTS OF GLASSPORT PA., CASCADE PARK, JULY 8, 09".
Clear $20-25 Stain $35-40 add 150% for advertising
Ref.- HC5 p. 152 (advertisement), KM6 plate 33 (only 4 piece table set shown)

477. **NEW HAMPSHIRE (BENT BUCKLE, U. S. GLASS' NO. 15084)**
2 1/4" dia. x 3 1/8" ht. or
3 1/4" dia. x 4 3/8" ht.
The U. S. Glass Co. was the maker of this pattern about 1903. It was made in clear, with rose stain and possibly ruby stain. The pattern contains over 55 different pieces.
Both Sizes Clear $20-25 Both Sizes Stain $40-50
Ref.- JLPG p. 383, MMPG p. 202

478. **HARVARD YARD**
3 1/8" dia. x 3 1/8" ht.
This pattern was made by the Tarentum Glass Co. about 1896. It was made in clear, green, pink and with gold. Lucas (TAR) shows a sugar and creamer with metal tops. The mug shown also has a metal base. They could have been part of a set. There are about 20 different items in the pattern.
Clear $25-30 Color $35-40
Ref.- TAR p. 300 (mug not listed)

479. **DIAMOND SPEARHEAD**
2 3/4" dia. x 2 7/8" ht.
Shards of this pattern were found at an old glass factory site in Indiana, Pa., which operated under several names. The pattern was introduced in 1900 as No. 22. The item shown is a souvenir dated 1900, so the maker would have been the National Glass Co., which was then operating the Northwood Glass Works. It was produced in clear, cobalt, green opalescent, blue opalescent and canary opalescent. Over 30 different pieces were manufactured in this pattern.
Clear $30-35 Canary and Green Opal $80-110 Cobalt and Blue Opal $125-150
Ref.- HC2 p. 19, HCO p. 58, HCP1 p. 14

480. **ARCHED FLEUR-DE-LIS**
2 7/8" dia. x 3 1/8" ht.
Bryce, Higbee & Co. was the maker of this pattern until 1907. After that, the J. B. Higbee Co. made it. It was produced in clear, ruby stain, and ruby stain with gold. Higbee did not decorate glass. It was probably stained by the Oriental Decorating Co. also of Pittsburgh. Over 40 different pieces were made in this pattern.
Clear $25-30 Stain $50-60
Ref.- JLPG p. 218, RS plate 7, PAT p. 223

481

482

483

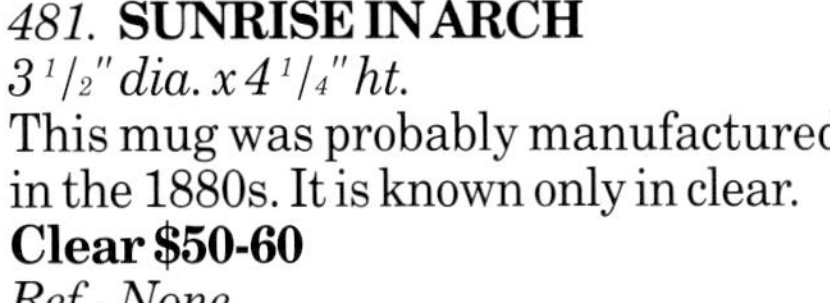
481. **SUNRISE IN ARCH**
3 1/2" dia. x 4 1/4" ht.
This mug was probably manufactured in the 1880s. It is known only in clear.
Clear $50-60
Ref.- None

482. **PENNY CANDY**
1 3/8" dia. x 2" ht.
This mug was made by the Federal Glass Co. It has the "F" in a shield trademark which was used after 1932. It was made in clear, dark amber and possibly other colors.
Clear $10-15 Amber $20-25
Ref.- None

483. **RISING SUN (SUNSHINE, U. S. GLASS' NO. 15110)**
2 7/8" dia. x 2 1/4" ht.
The U. S. Glass Co. was the maker of this pattern about 1908. A punch cup or custard is shown. It was produced in clear, with gold and with stained suns in rose, green, blue or yellow.
Clear $15-20 Stain $20-25
Ref.- HC7 p. 186

484. **MINNESOTA (MUCHNESS, U. S. GLASS' NO. 15055)**
2 3/4" dia. x 3 1/4" ht.
The U. S. Glass Co. made this pattern about 1898. It was produced in clear, with gold, green and scarce in ruby stain. The pattern has over 85 different pieces.
Clear $20-25 Green $35-40 Stain $40-45
Ref.- HC5 p. 152 (advertisement), JLPG p. 371

484

485

486

487

488

489

490

491

492

493

485. **PANAMA (FINECUT BAR, U. S. GLASS' NO. 15088)**
2 7/8" dia. x 3 1/8" ht.
The U. S. Glass Co. was the maker of this pattern about 1904. It was made in clear only. Over 25 different pieces were made in this pattern.
Clear $25-30
Ref.- WEPG p. 419 (mug not listed)

486. **PANELLED PALM (U. S. GLASS' NO. 15095)**
2 7/8" dia. x 3 3/8" ht.
The U. S. Glass Co. made this pattern about 1906. It was manufactured in clear, rose stain, yellow stain, amethyst stain and ruby stain.
Clear $35-40 Stain $50-60
Ref.- HC5 p. 43 (mug not listed)

487. **SCRAMBLED WHEELS**
This stein was probably made after 1900. It was only produced in clear.
Clear $15-20
Ref.- MET2 p. 205, TOY p. 138

488. **TENNESSEE (JEWEL & CRESENT, U. S. GLASS' NO. 15064)**
3" dia. x 3 5/8" ht.
The U. S. Glass Co. was the maker of this pattern about 1899. It was made in clear and with colored jewels. Over 25 different pieces were made in this pattern.
Clear $40-50 Stain $60-75
Ref.- A&C2 p. 243 (advertisement) HC5 p. 147 (advertisement), JLPG p. 507, MMPG p. 80

489. **FLEUR-DE-LIS & DRAPE (U. S. GLASS' NO. 15009)**
mustard or cup and saucer: 2 7/8" dia. x 2 3/4" ht.
This pattern was manufactured by Adams & Co. in the 1880s. After 1891, it was made by the U. S. Glass Co. There is a cup and saucer and a mustard. It was made in clear, green and opaque white with gold. There are over 30 different pieces in the pattern.
Clear $40-45 Color $65-80 without saucer 50% less and 50% more with cover
Ref.- HC5 p. 61 (advertisement), MET1 p. 139, MMPG p. 242, PG&B p. 19 (advertisement)

494

495

490. **WYOMING (ENIGMA, U. S. GLASS' NO. 15081)**
2 3/4" dia. x 3 7/8" ht.
The U. S. Glass Co. made this pattern about 1903. It was only produced in clear. There are over 35 different items in this pattern.
Clear $40-50
Ref.- JLPG p. 563

491. **PARIS (ZIPPER CROSS)**
2 7/8" dia. x 3 1/8" ht.
Bryce, Higbee & Co. made this mug until 1907. At that time the J. B. Higbee Glass Co. took over production. After 1918, it was manufactured by the New Martinsville Glass Manufacturing Co. It appears that they and the Paden City Glass Manufacturing Co. bought several of the Higbee molds after Higbee went out of business in 1918. The mug was shown in a 1901 Ward's catalogue. It was made only in clear. There are over 75 different items in the pattern.
Clear $25-30
Ref.- NM p. 30 (advertisement), WHPG p. 198

492. **PALM LEAF FAN**
2 3/4" dia. x 3 1/8" ht.
Bryce, Higbee & Co. manufactured this pattern about 1905. It is shown in a 1905 Montgomery Ward catalogue. It was produced in clear and is rare in ruby stain. There are over 50 diverse items in the pattern.
Clear $25-30
Ref.- HCP1 p. 7 (advertisement, but no mug)

493. **PATTEE CROSS (U. S. GLASS' NO. 15112)**
2 1/2" dia. x 3 3/8" ht.
The U. S. Glass Co. manufactured this pattern about 1909. It was produced in clear, green and amethyst stain. The table service contains over 40 items.
Clear $20-25
Green and Stain $35-40
Ref.- MMPG p. 142 (mug not listed)

494. **PRINCE OF WALES PLUME**
3 1/8" dia. x 2 1/4" ht.
The A. H. Heisey Glass Co. was the maker of this pattern about 1902. A punch cup is shown. It was made in clear with gold, green with gold and ruby stain.
Clear $10-15
Green & Stain $25-30
Ref.- HSY p. 50

495. **BIJOU (FAN WITH ACANTHUS LEAF)**
3" dia. x 3 1/4" ht.
The Greensburg Glass Co. made this pattern in the 1880s. It is known only in clear.
Clear $30-35
Ref.- KM2 p. 125, KM8 p. 62, 151 and 152 (advertisement, but no mug shown)

496. **MEDALLION**
p. 147 for pattern picture
The U. S. Glass Co. made this pattern after 1891. It was probably made by one of the merger factories in the 1880s. It was made in clear, amber, blue, apple green and canary. The pattern has about 20 different pieces in all colors.
Clear $20-25 Color $35-40
Ref.- MMPG p. 164

497. **PURITAN, ROBINSON'S**
not shown
This pattern was made by the Robinson Glass Co. of Zanesville, Ohio, about 1894. It was produced in clear, but items may be found in ruby-stain or amber-stain.
Clear $20-25
Ref.- KM6 plate 39 (advertisement)

RIBS

498. **DUNCAN'S NO. 904**
2 7/8" dia. x 3 1/4" ht.
George Duncan & Sons was the maker of this mug in the 1880s. After 1891, it was made by the U. S. Glass Co. It was produced in clear and ruby stain.
Clear $20-25 Stain $30-35
Ref. MMPG p. 426

499. **OVERALL LATTICE (INDIANA'S NO. 38)**
2 1/4" dia. x 3 3/8" ht.
The Indiana Tumbler & Goblet Co. was the manufacturer of this pattern in 1897. After 1899, it was made by the National Glass Co. Then after 1907, it was made by the Indiana Glass Co. The mug is shown in a 1907-08 Indiana Glass Co. catalogue. The mug was made in souvenired ruby stain.
Stain $35-40
Ref.- GRE p. 50, GREE fig.30 and 277 (advertisement), HC7 p. 166

500. **TRUNCATED CUBE (THOMPSON'S NO. 77)**
2 5/8" dia. x 4" ht.
The Thompson Glass Co. made this pattern about 1892. This is a water tumbler with an applied handle. It was made in clear and ruby stain. The ruby stain is often souvenired. Many of these items were souvenired after the factory closed. About 20 different items were made in this pattern.
Clear $40-50 Stain $60-75
Ref.- JLPG p. 528 (mug not listed)

501. **BEATTY RIB**
2 1/2" dia. x 3 1/4" ht.
The pattern was made by A. J. Beatty & Co. about 1888. It was produced in white and blue opalescent. Over 35 different pieces were made in this pattern. It is possible that this and #499 are the same mug, but the ribs on the drawing taper to a point and the handles are slightly different.
White Opal. $30-35
Blue Opal. $50-60
Ref.- GCF1 p. 92, HC2 p. 18, MET1 p. 101 PG&B p. 58 (advertisement)

498

499

500

501

502

503

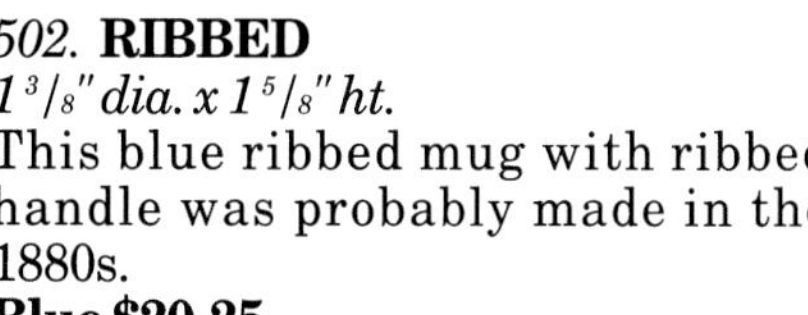

502. **RIBBED**
1 3/8" dia. x 1 5/8" ht.
This blue ribbed mug with ribbed handle was probably made in the 1880s.
Blue $20-25
Ref.- None

503. **SPLIT RIB**
2 7/8" dia. x 3 3/8" ht.
This mug was probably made in the 1880s. It is known only in opaque white and opaque blue.
Color $30-35
Ref.- OPA plate 180

504

505

506

507

504. **SPEAR**
A. J. Beatty & Sons manufactured this mug in the late 1880s. After 1891, it was manufactured by the U. S. Glass Co. It is known only in clear. It looks similar to Beatty Rib.
Clear $25-30
Ref.- HOB1, PG&B p. 58 (advertisement), TOY p. 157 (advertisement)

505. **STARS & STRIPES (KOKOMO'S NO. 209)**
custard cup or mug: $2^{1}/_{4}$" dia. x $3^{1}/_{8}$" ht.
The Kokomo Glass Co. was the manufacturer of this pattern about 1900. It was also made by the Federal Glass Co. about 1914. It was produced in clear and opaque white. It is shown in an 1899 Montgomery Ward catalogue under the name Brilliant. There are about 20 different pieces in the pattern.
Clear Mug $20-25 Opaque White Mug $30-35 Clear Cup $10-15 Opaque White Cup $15-20
Ref.- GCF1 p. 84, JJ p. 20, JLPG p. 492, TOY p. 155

506. **RIBBED PANELS**
$2^{3}/_{4}$" dia. x $2^{7}/_{8}$" ht.
This mug was probably made about 1890. The panels between the ribs are frosted and so is the bottom.
Frosted $25-30
Ref.- None

507. **PLEATED SKIRT**
$2^{1}/_{8}$" dia. x $3^{3}/_{8}$" ht.
This mug was probably made after 1900. It was produced in clear, green, cobalt, custard and alabaster. When it is souvenired, it is decorated with enameled flowers.
Clear $15-20 Color $25-30
Ref.- GCF1 p. 89

508. **NOTCHED DIAMOND RIB (BELLAIRE'S NO. 438)**
2 1/4" dia. x 3 1/2" ht.
The Bellaire Goblet Co. was the maker of this mug about 1898. The shape is very similar to mugs made by the Indiana Glass Co. and the National Glass Co. at Greentown, IN. after the turn of the century. It was made in clear and ruby stain.
Clear $15-20 Stain $30-35
Ref.- FINP p. 48

509. **SERRATED PRISM**
2 1/4" dia. x 3 1/8" ht.
The National Glass Co. was the maker of this mug about 1900. It was made only in clear.
Clear $15-20
Ref.- HCG1 p. 77, WEPG p. 411 (mug not listed)

510. **PANELLED DEWDROP**
3 3/8" dia. x 3 5/8" ht.
This pattern was designed and patented by Henry Franz on June 25, 1878 and assigned to Campbell, Jones & Co. This mug is a water tumbler with an applied handle. It was made only in clear. The pattern has over 25 different pieces.
Clear $35-40
Ref.- PG &B p. 98 (mug not mentioned), WHPG p. 191

511. **LITTLE PRISM**
1 1/2" dia. x 2" ht.
This mug was probably manufactured about the turn of the century. It was made only in clear.
Clear $10-15
Ref.- None

512

512

513

514

515

516

512. **ROMAN ROSETTE (U. S. GLASS' NO. 15030)**
2 1/2" dia. x 3" ht. or larger
Bryce, Walker & Co. made this pattern from about 1875. In 1882, Bryce Brothers took over production. The U.S. Glass Co. continued production after 1891. It was manufactured in clear, and ruby stain. Over 25 different pieces were produced in this pattern.
Both Sizes Clear $35-40
Both Sizes Stain $50-60
Ref.- HC7 p. 27, JLPG p. 450, MMPG p. 32, WHPG p. 223

513. **ROMAN ROSETTE, LATE (NEW YORK)**
2 1/4" dia. x 3 1/2" ht. or smaller (2 oz.)
The McKee Glass Co. and the Westmoreland Specialty Co. made this mug about the turn of the century. It was produced in clear, amber and blue.
Both Sizes Clear $30-35 Both Sizes Color $40-45
Ref.- GCF1 p. 85, MMPG p. 282, TOY p. 154

514. **PANELS**
2 3/8" dia. x 3 3/8" ht.
The Westmoreland Specialty Co. was the maker of this mug about 1915. There are 16 concave panels. It is known only in cobalt. This mug has been seen with a cardboard seal in the mouth. It was to contain candy.
Cobalt $35-40
Ref.- TOY p. 139

515. **COLUMNS**
2 1/2" dia. x 2 3/4" ht.
This mug is probably from the 1880s. There are 22 convex columns. It was made in clear, blue and possibly other colors. This mug has been seen with a cardboard seal in the mouth. It was to contain candy.
Clear $15-20 Blue $25-30
Ref.- DAZ

516. **DOUBLE BEETLE BAND**
1 5/8" dia. x 2 1/4" ht. or 2" dia. x 2 3/4" ht. or 2 3/4" dia. x 3 3/4" ht.
The Columbia Glass Co. was the maker of this pattern about 1888. It was produced in clear, amber, blue and canary. Over 25 different pieces were made in this pattern.
All Sizes in Clear $25-35 All Sizes in Color $40-55
Ref.- FIN p. 67

518

519

520

521

PANELS

517. **ENCORE**
not shown
This souvenired mug was made after 1910. It was produced only in marigold carnival.
Marigold $65-80
Ref.- None

518. **COLONIAL, HIGBEE (ESTELLE, PADEN CITY'S NO. 205)**
custard cup or mug: 3" dia. x 2 7/8" ht.
This pattern was made by the J. B. Higbee Glass Co. about 1910. It is listed, but not shown in a trade catalogue from Jan., 1910. After 1918, it was made by the Paden City Glass Manufacturing Co. It appears that they and the New Martinsville Glass Manufacturing Co. bought many of the Higbee molds after Higbee went out of business. The mug and several of the other items have the Higbee trademark, a bee with "H I G" on the wings and body. It was produced in clear only. There are over 50 different items in the pattern.
Clear Mug $20-25 Clear Cup $10-15
Ref.- PC p. 41 (mug not listed)

519. **MEDIUM FLAT PANEL**
3 1/8" dia. x 3 1/2" ht.
The A. H. Heisey Glass Co. was the maker of this mug about 1908. It has 9 panels and is clear.
Clear $20-25
Ref.- HSY p. 23

520. **ORIENTAL PENNY CANDY**
1 5/8" dia. x 2" ht.
This mug was made by the Westmoreland Specialty Co. about 1905. It was produced in custard, opaque green, opaque blue and ruby stain.
Color $10-15 Stain $15-20
Ref.- TOY p. 140

522

523

524

525

521. **PANELLED 44 (ATHENIA, U. S. GLASS' NO. 15140)**
$2^{7}/_{8}$"dia. x $3^{5}/_{8}$"ht. or larger
The U. S. Glass Co. was the maker of this pattern about 1912. It was produced in clear with gold, with platinum, green stain and amethyst stain. Over 40 different pieces were made in this pattern.
Small Clear with Gold and Platinum $35-45
Small Stain $50-60
Large Clear with Gold and Platinum $75-95
Ref.- MMPG p. 248, PP2 p. 127

522. **PORTLAND (U. S. GLASS' NO. 15121)**
$3^{1}/_{8}$"dia. x 3"ht.
The U. S. Glass Co. made this pattern in the 1890s. The pattern has over 30 different items. It was produced in clear and ruby stain.
Clear $25-30 Stain $50-65
Ref.- WHPG p. 26

523. **ZIPPERED CORNERS**
$2^{1}/_{8}$"dia. x $2^{7}/_{8}$"ht.
This pattern was probably manufactured by the National Glass Co. about 1900. It was made in clear and ruby stain.
Clear $20-25 Stain $30-35
Ref.- HC7 p. 219

524. **PENNY CANDY**
$1^{5}/_{8}$"dia. x 2"ht.
The 1914 Federal Glass Co. Packer's Catalogue shows this mug. It is known in amber, cobalt, souvenired ruby stain and was possibly made in other colors. There are at least 2 mold variations and it has been reproduced.
Cobalt and Stain $15-20
Ref.- HGC5 p. 40 (advertisement), TOY p. 140

525. **OLD COLUMBIA (PRISM BUTTRESS)**
This mug was manufactured by the Columbia Glass Co. about 1890. After 1891, it was made by the U. S. Glass Co. It was made in clear and green.
Clear $15-20 Green $30-35
Ref.- FIN p. 33, HCG1 p. 12 (advertisement),

526. **COLONIAL, IMPERIAL (IMPERIAL'S NO. 3)**
2 7/8"dia. x 5"ht.
The Imperial Glass Co. was the maker of this pattern after 1910. They made a vase, a toothpick, an open sugar, and a candlestick as well as this lemonade. It was also made in carnival colors: marigold, amethyst and green. The lemonade is known only in marigold.
Marigold $50-60
Ref.-CARN p. 44

527. **GOLDEN OXEN**
2 7/8"dia. x 5 1/4"ht.
This stein was manufactured after 1910. It was made in only in marigold carnival.
Marigold $40-50
Ref.- CARN p. 90

528. **NOTCHED PANELS (SERRATED PRISM)**
2 1/4"dia. x 3 3/8"ht.
The D. C. Jenkins Glass Co. was the manufacturer of this mug after 1906. There are 12 panels. It was made in clear and ruby stain.
Clear $20-25 Stain $30-35
Ref.- MET1 p. 170 (mug not listed)

529. **TRIUMPH**
2 5/8"dia. x 3 3/4"ht.
This mug was made in the 1890s. There are 14 thumbprint panels around the base. This ruby-stained example is a souvenir.
Stain $15-20
Ref.- HCT fig.248

530. **NAIL (U. S. GLASS' NO. 15002)**
2 5/8"dia. x 3 5/8"ht.
This pattern was manufactured by Ripley & Co. in the 1880s. After 1891, it was made by the U. S. Glass Co. It was produced in clear and ruby stain. There are over 30 different items in the pattern.
Clear $40-45 Stain $60-70
Ref.- JLPG p. 378 (mug not listed)

531

532

533

534

535

SQUARES / RECTANGLES

531. **HANOVER**
smaller or 2 5/8"dia. x 3"ht.
The Richards & Hartley Glass Co. was the maker of these mugs about 1888. The U. S. Glass Co. made it after 1891. There are about 30 different pieces in the pattern. They were produced in clear, amber, blue and canary.
Both Sizes Clear $20-25
Both Sizes Color $35-40
Ref.- JLPG p. 262, PG&B p. 286 (advertisement), TAR p. 210 (advertisement)

532. **HIDALGO (FROSTED WAFFLE)**
3 1/8"dia. x 2 5/8"ht.
Adams & Co. made this pattern in the 1880s. The U. S. Glass Co. made it after 1891. The item of interest is a cup and saucer. It was produced in frosted, amber and ruby stain.
Frosted $35-45 Amber and Stain $50-60 50% less without saucer
Ref.- HC5 p. 68 (advertisement), JLPG p. 274, WHPG p. 141

533. **MITERED BLOCK**
1 1/2"dia. x 1 1/2"ht.
A. J. Beatty & Sons was the maker of this mug in the 1880s. It is known only in clear.
Clear $20-25
Ref.- GCF1 p. 87, PG&B p. 60 (advertisement)

534. **REEDED WAFFLE (BERLIN, BRYCE BROTHERS' NO. 87)**
2 1/2"dia. x 3" ht.
Bryce Brothers made this mug in the 1880s. The U. S. Glass Co. made it after 1891. A goblet is also known. It was produced in clear only.
Clear $20-25
Ref.- HOB1, PG&B p. 86 (advertisement)

535. **BARREL BLOCK (GREENSBURG'S NO. 130)**
2 1/2"dia. x 3 1/8" ht.
The pattern is shown in an 1899 Greensburg Glass Co. catalogue. It was made only in clear.
Clear $25-30
Ref.- KM5 plate 7 (advertisement, but no mug)

536. **GREEK KEY (U. S. SHERATON, U. S. GLASS' NO. 15144)**
2 1/2"dia. x 3 3/4"ht.
This pattern was made by the U. S. Glass Co. about 1912. It was produced in clear, with gold, with platinum and light green.
Clear $20-25
Ref.- HC5 p. 158 (advertisement, no mug shown), MMPG p. 466

536

537

538

540

542

537. **GREEK KEY VARIANT**
$2^1/_4$"dia. x $3^3/_8$"ht.
This mug was probably made at the end of the 19th century. It is known only in clear.
Clear $20-25
Ref.- None

538. **BLOCK & JEWEL**
$2^1/_4$"dia. x $3^3/_4$"ht. or
$2^1/_4$"dia. x $3^3/_8$"ht.
This mug was probably manufactured in the 1890s. It was made in clear and opaque white.
Clear $20-25 Opaque White $30-35
Ref.- OPA plate 82

539. **TWO PANEL**
p. 147 for pattern picture
The Richards & Hartley Flint Glass Co. manufactured this pattern in the 1880s. The U. S. Glass Co. made it after 1891. It was made in clear, amber, blue, apple green and canary. Over 35 different items were produced in the pattern in all of the colors.
Clear $20-25 Color $30-40
Ref.- JLPG p. 532, LEE p. 513

540. **DUNCAN BLOCK**
$2^5/_8$"dia. x $3^1/_2$"ht.
This pattern was made by George Duncan & Sons in the 1880s and was made by the U. S. Glass Co. after 1891. It is known only in clear. There are over 25 different items in the pattern.
Clear $25-30
Ref.- HC5 p. 98 (advertisement, no mug shown)

541. **CATHEDRAL (ORION)**
p. 147 for pattern picture
Bryce Brothers was the maker of this pattern in the 1880s. After 1891, it was manufactured by the U. S. Glass Co. The mug was made in clear and ruby stain. The rest of the pattern was produced in amber, blue, amethyst and canary as well. The ruby stain was only produced by the U. S. Glass Co. Over 55 different items were made in this pattern.
Clear $20-25 Stain $30-35
Ref.- JLPG p. 112

542. **DIVIDED BLOCK WITH SUNBURST (MAJESTIC)**
mug- $2^1/_4$"dia. x $3^3/_8$"ht. or cup and saucer: $2^1/_2$"dia. x $2^1/_4$"ht.
McKee & Brothers, the National Glass Co. and the Cambridge Glass Co. were all the makers of this pattern about 1900. It was made in clear, and ruby stain. It is rare in green, cobalt, and yellow-green.
Clear $20-25 Stain $35-40
Color $40-50
50% less without saucer
Ref.- GCF1 p. 88, TOY p. 154
NO CHOCOLATE!!!!!!

543. **KLONDIKE (DALZELL'S NO. 75)**
not shown
This pattern was manufactured by the Dalzell, Gilmore & Leighton Glass Co. about 1898. It was made to celebrate the Klondike gold rush. The items of interest are a cup and saucer. According to an advertisement, 40 different pieces were made in the pattern. Most have a rectangular form. They were made in clear, amber stained stripes and acid frosted with amber stained stripes.
Clear $50-60 Stain $150-175
Frosted with Stain $200-250
Ref.- HCG1 p. 15 (advertisement, but no mug), JLPG p. 316

542

544

545

544. **BASKETWEAVE**
$2^{3}/_{8}$"dia. x $2^{1}/_{2}$"ht.
The shape and size of the cup and saucer indicates the maker may have been the Columbia Glass Co. about 1890. They were made in clear, amber, blue, apple green and canary. The pattern has over 30 different pieces. The water tray has a rural scene.
Clear $40-45 Color $50-60 without saucer 50% less
Ref.- GCF p. 51, MET1 p. 163, TOY p. 133, WHPG p. 30

545. **BEATTY HONEYCOMB**
$2^{1}/_{2}$"dia. x $3^{1}/_{4}$"ht.
The pattern was made by A. J. Beatty & Co. about 1888. It was produced in white opalescent, blue opalescent and lavender opalescent. The pattern has over 40 different items.
White Opal. $35-40
Blue Opal. $45-55
Ref.- HC2 p. 18

546. **STARS & BARS**
3"dia. x $2^{3}/_{8}$"ht.
This custard or punch cup was manufactured by the Bellaire Goblet Co. about 1890. It was made in clear, amber and blue.
Clear $15-20 Color $25-30
Ref.- FIN p. 51

547. **LOG & STAR (CUBE & DIAMOND)**
2"dia. x $2^{1}/_{4}$"ht. or $2^{1}/_{4}$"dia. x $2^{5}/_{8}$"ht. or 3"dia. x $3^{1}/_{2}$"ht.
These mugs were made by the Bellaire Goblet Co. about 1890. They were produced in clear, amber and blue.
All Sizes in Clear $20-25 All Sizes in Color $30-40
Ref.- FIN p. 51 (advertisement), MET1 p. 165, PG&B p. 66 (advertisement), TOY p. 157, WEPG p. 243

548. **FLARED BOTTOM SQUARES**
$1^{7}/_{8}$"dia. x $2^{3}/_{8}$"ht.
This mug was probably manufactured after 1900. It was made in clear, amber and blue.
Clear $15-20 Color $25-30
Ref.- GCF2 p. 190

547

546

548

549

550

551

552

549. **SIMPLICITY**
2 5/8"dia. x 2"ht. or 2 5/8"dia. x 3"ht.
This mug was probably made in the 1880s. It was made in clear, blue, and amethyst.
Clear $25-30 Color $60-80
Ref.- None

550. **BASKETWEAVE VARIANT**
1 7/8"dia. x 2 1/4"ht.
Bryce Brothers was the maker of this pattern in the 1880s. After 1891, it was manufactured by the U. S. Glass Co. There is a finger lamp with a basket to hold matches as well as this mug. This mug is probably a match holder. It was made in clear, amber, blue, apple green and canary.
Clear $20-25 Color $30-35
Ref.- PG&B p. 90 (advertisement)

551. **THREE STORY (PERSIAN)**
3"dia. x 3 1/4"ht.
Bryce, Higbee & Co. was the maker of this pattern about 1885. It was produced in clear, amber and blue. There are over 35 different pieces in the pattern.
Clear $25-30 Color $35-45
Ref.- KM8 p. 122 and 136 (advertisement), LEE p. 511, MET1 p. 159, MMPG p. 66, WHPG p. 201

552. **BLOCKED THUMBPRINT BAND**
2 3/4"dia. x 3 1/4"ht.
The Duncan & Miller Glass Co. was the manufacturer of this pattern in the early 1900s. It was made in clear, custard and ruby stain. The ruby stained items are souvenired.
Clear $10-15
Custard and Stain $20-25
Ref.- MMPG p. 38

SWIRLS, ROPE, DRAPE, STARS, HEARTS, TEXTURES & MISC.

553. **SWIRL, NORTHWOOD**
not shown
This pattern may have been made by the H. Northwood Co. There is also a water set in the pattern. Tumblers are marked with the underlined "N" in a circle trademark, but the mug is not. The mug was produced in marigold carnival. Other items were made in green carnival and amethyst carnival.
Marigold $60-70
Ref.- CARN p. 198

554. **BEADED SWIRL & DISC**
2 3/4"dia. x 2 7/8"ht. (saucer not shown)
This pattern was made by the U. S. Glass Co. about 1904. The items of interest here are a cup and saucer. It was produced in clear, amber stained discs, blue and amber stain and yellow and fuchsia stain. These stains are intense together. The pattern was manufactured with over 25 different pieces.
Clear $40-50 Stain $100-125 without saucer 50% less
Ref.- MMPG p. 490 (mug not listed)

555. **RAY**
2 5/8"dia. x 3 5/8"ht.
McKee & Brothers shows this mug in a catalogue from about 1894. Our picture shows a packer's cover. It was made only in clear.
Clear $20-25 add 50% for cover
Ref.- TOY p. 158 (advertisement)

556. **SWIRL BAND**
3"dia. x 3 1/2"ht.
This pattern was probably made by the Burlington Glass Works in the 1880s. It was produced clear and etched. There is at least a 4 piece table set and a goblet as well as a mug.
Clear $20-25
Ref.- MMPG p. 484 (mug not listed)

557. **BEADED SWIRL**
2 1/4"dia. x 3 3/8"ht.
This pattern was made by George Duncan's Sons in the 1880s and by the U. S. Glass Co. after 1891. It was produced in clear, light green, dark green and with gold. The light green is scarce. There are about 45 different items in the pattern.
Clear $15-20 Color $25-30
Ref.- MET2 p. 111 (mug not listed)

558. **PURITAN, WESTMORELAND'S**
1 1/2"dia. x 1 3/4"ht. or
2 1/8"dia. x 3 1/8"ht.
The Westmoreland Specialty Co. made these mugs about 1910. They were produced in clear, sapphire blue, amethyst, yellowish green and dark brown. These mugs are incorrectly called Rea in TOY and GCF1.
Both Sizes Clear $20-25 Both Sizes Color $30-40
Ref.- HCG1 p. 82, HCG3 p. 34

559. **ZIPPER SWIRL**
2 3/8"dia. x 3 1/8"ht.
This mug was probably made about 1890. It is known only in clear.
Clear $20-25
Ref.- None

560. **BEADED SWIRL VARIANT**
1 3/8"dia. x 1 3/4"ht.
This mug was probably manufactured in the 1880s. It was made only in clear.
Clear $20-25
Ref.- GCF1 p. 93

561. **LUTZ (BALL & SWIRL VARIANT)**
2 1/4"dia. x 3 3/8"ht.
This mug was made by McKee & Brothers about 1894. It was produced in clear only.
All Sizes Clear $20-25
Ref.- MMPG plate 237

562. **BALL & SWIRL**
2 1/8"dia. x 3 1/8"ht. or
2 1/2"dia. x 4 1/4"ht. or
2 3/4"dia. x 3 5/8"ht.
This mug is shown in a McKee & Brothers catalogue from about 1894. It was made in clear, ruby stain, marigold carnival, opaque white and with gold. The pattern has about 30 different items.
All Sizes Clear $20-25
All Sizes Marigold $70-90
All Sizes Stain $30-35
Ref.- PG&B p. 57 (advertisement), JLPG p. 38, TOY p. 158 (advertisement), WHPG p. 24

563. **HEART & THUMBPRINT**
2 5/8"dia. x 2 1/8"ht.
The Tarentum Glass Co. was the manufacturer of this pattern about 1900. A cup and saucer is shown. It is known in clear, green and ruby stain with odd pieces in pink, custard and opaque green. Over 45 different items were made in this pattern.
Clear $35-45
Color and Stain $60-75
50% less without saucer
Ref.- JLPG p. 267, KM6 plate 51 (advertisement)

554

555

556

557

558

559

560

561

562

563

564. **BAR & SWIRL**
2 3/8" dia. x 3 5/8" ht.
This mug was probably made in the 1890s and is known only in opaque white.
Opaque White $25-30
Ref.- MET1 p. 145, OPA plate 195

565. **ROPE**
2 1/4"dia. x 3 5/8"ht.
This opaque white mug was probably made in the 1890s.
Opaque White $25-30
Ref.- OPA p. 189

566. **SWIRL**
This mug was probably manufactured in the 1880s. It was made in clear, opaque blue and possibly opaque white.
Clear $20-25 Color $30-35
Ref.- TOY p. 140

567. **BRITTANIC**
p. 147 for pattern picture
This pattern was made by McKee & Brothers in the 1880s and by the National Glass Co. after 1899. It was produced in clear, ruby stain, amber stain and green. The pattern was made with over 55 different items.
Clear $20-25
Green and Stain $35-45
Ref.- JLPG p. 80, RS plate 11

568. **SWIRL & CABLE**
The Dalzell, Gilmore & Leighton Glass Co. was the maker of this mug about 1891. It is shown in a spring 1893 Butler Brother catalogue. It is known only in clear.
Clear $25-30
Ref.- FIN p. 87, FINP p. 68, GCF2 p. 190

569. **BALL & SWIRL VARIANT**
not shown
This mug is similar to Ball & Swirl, except it has no ring around the top and has a notched handle. It is shown in a 1907-08 Indiana Glass Co. catalogue. It was produced in clear only.
Clear $20-25
Ref.- GREE plate 277 (advertisement)

570. **REA (BEADED SWIRL)**
not shown
A. J. Beatty & Sons made these mugs in the 1880s. They produced made only in clear. This mug is similar to Westmoreland's Puritan, except without a beaded handle.
Clear $20-25
Ref.- PG&B p. 57 (advertisement)

571. **BEATTY SWIRL**
not shown
The pattern was made by A. J. Beatty & Co. about 1888. It was produced in white opalescent and blue opalescent. The pattern was made with over 35 different pieces.
White Opal. $35-40
Blue Opal. $45-55
Ref.- HC2 p. 18

572. **CURTAIN (SULTAN)**
3 1/8"dia. x 3 3/4"ht.
Bryce Brothers was the maker of this pattern in the 1880s. It was made in clear and is rare in amber. It was possibly made in blue. The pattern has over 30 different pieces.
Clear $30-35 Amber $50-60
Ref. JLPG p. 144, MMPG p. 496

564

565

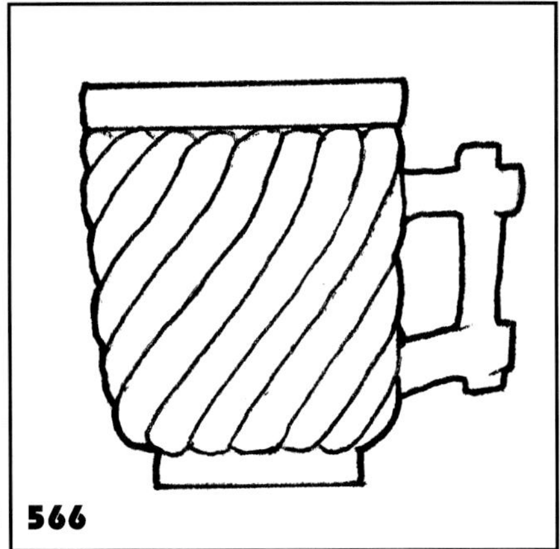
566

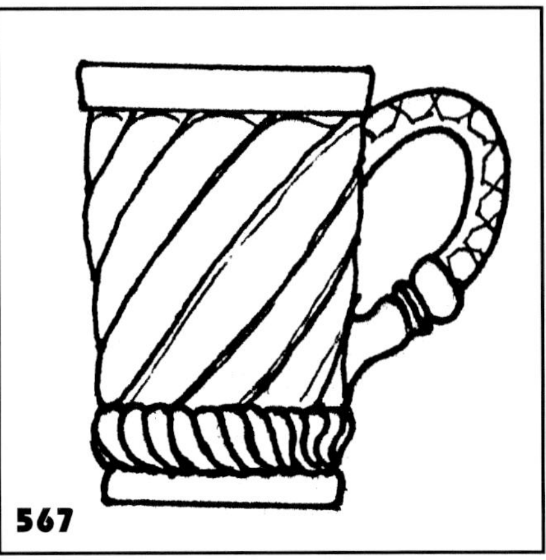
567

572

573

574

575

575

577

578

573. **SHELL BAND**
2 3/4"dia. x 3"ht.
This mug was probably made about 1890. It is known only in aqua slag.
Slag $60-75
Ref.- None

574. **HEART BAND (McKEE'S NO. 139)**
2 7/8"dia. x 2 7/8"ht. or 2 7/8"dia. x 3 3/8"ht. or 2 7/8"dia. x 3 7/8"ht.
The McKee Glass Co. was the manufacturer of this pattern about 1897. Only the mugs, a creamer, a salt shaker, a sugar and a tumbler were made. Most items found are souvenired. It was made in clear, green, ruby stain, with gold and with enameled decoration. Also, made in carnival colors: marigold, aqua and green.
Both Sizes Clear and Enamel $20-25
Both Sizes Green and Stain $35-45
Ref.- MK p. 146 (advertisement), WHPG p. 137

575. **OVERSHOT**
many sizes and shapes
Overshot was made by the Portland Glass Co., the Boston & Sandwich Glass Co., in England and in Czechoslovakia. Technically, this is not pattern glass. Items are blown or mold blown. The gather of glass is rolled in fine glass shards, formed, then reheated. This gives an uneven surface to the glass. Items with applied snakes are rare. Mugs come in many shapes and sizes. It is shown here so that the difference can be seen between it and Tree of Life. The two are often confused. It was made in clear and colors. Over 100 different items were made in this technique.
Clear $50-60 Color $100-125
Ref.- KM6 plate 101 (advertisement without mug), MET2 p. 50 (mug not listed)

576. **FEATHER DUSTER (U. S. GLASS' NO. 15043)**
p. 147 for pattern picture
The U. S. Glass Co. was the maker of this pattern about 1895. It was produced in clear and green. The table service consists mostly of bowls and compotes. Over 55 different items were made in this pattern with the rarest being the McKinley Gold Standard bread plate.
Clear $15-20 Green $30-35
Ref.- JLPG p. 206

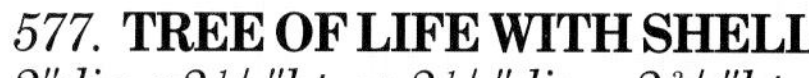
577. **TREE OF LIFE WITH SHELL**
2"dia. x 2 1/8"ht. or 2 1/2"dia. x 2 3/4"ht. or 3 1/8"dia. x 3 1/2"ht.
Many feel this mug is part of the Shell & Tassel pattern. If so, it was probably made by the Portland Glass Co. about 1870 or by George Duncan & Sons in the 1880s. However, there are not enough of this pattern's characteristics in the mug to say for sure. The mug was made in clear, blue and is rare in amber.
All Sizes in Clear $65-90
All Sizes in Blue $100-120
All Sizes in Amber $125-150
Ref.- TOY p. 30 and 140

579

580

581

582

583

584

578. **STAR & IVY**
$2^3/_8$"dia. x $2^5/_8$"ht.
This cup and saucer was made by the Model Flint Glass Co. in the 1890s. 2 mold variations are known. It is known in clear, light amber, dark amber and blue.
Clear $40-50 Color $60-75
without saucer 50% less
Ref.- ALB p. 57 (advertisement), FIN p. 129 (advertisement), FINP p. 87, MET2 p. 207, TOY p. 133

579. **DRAPE**
$2^1/_4$"dia. x $3^1/_8$"ht.
This mug was probably made in the 1890s. It was produced in clear with gold.
Clear $20-25
Ref.- GCF2 p. 188

580. **DRUM**
$1^7/_8$"dia. x 2"ht.
Bryce, Higbee & Co. made this pattern in the 1880s. There is a children's four piece table set and a mustard as well as a mug. It was produced in clear and is scarce in color.
Clear $35-40
Ref.- GCF1 p. 59, HCT p. 79, TOY p. 152, WHPG p. 100

581. **CAPITAL (FILAGREE, ESTATE when carnival)**
$2^3/_4$"dia. x $2^7/_8$"ht.
The Westmoreland Specialty Co. was the maker of this mug about 1907. A 1907 Butler Brothers catalogue shows this mug. It was made in clear with silver or gold and marigold carnival. Also known in souvenired.
Clear $15-20 Marigold $70-90
Ref.- HCG2 p. 66 (advertisement)

582. **FISHSCALE (CORAL)**
$3^1/_8$"dia. x $3^3/_4$"ht.
Bryce Brothers made the pattern about 1888. After 1891, it was made by the U.S. Glass Co. It's known in clear and is rare in ruby stain. The pattern has about 50 different items.
Clear $40-50
Ref.- JLPG p. 216, LEE p. 498, PG&B p. 86 (advertisement)

583. **DOUBLE THREADS**
2"dia. x $3^1/_2$"ht.
This mug with threading at the top and the bottom is a lemonade. It was probably made in the 1890s. It is known only in clear.
Clear $35-40
Ref.- None

584. **STAR & LINES**
$2^1/_4$"dia. x $3^3/_8$"ht.
This mug may have been made by the Westmoreland Specialty Co. in the early 1900s. It is known only in clear.
Clear $20-25
Ref.- None

585

586

587

588

589

589

585. **GOTHIC ARCH & HEART**
2 1/4"dia. x 2 3/8"ht. or
2 5/8"dia. x 3 1/2"ht.
This mug was made in France about 1880. It is known only in clear.
Both Sizes Clear $25-35
Ref.- None

586. **CORD & TASSEL**
3 3/8"dia. x 3 5/8"ht.
The LaBelle Glass Co. originally was the maker of this pattern in the 1870s. It was made only in clear. The pattern has about 25 different pieces. Andrew H. Baggs designed and patented the pattern on July 23, 1872. After his patent expired, the Central Glass Co. issued its own version in 1876. The mug is rare.
Clear $80-100
Ref.- JLPG p. 130, MET1 p. 131, MET2 p. 195

587. **SKEWED HONEYCOMB**
2 3/4"dia. x 3 1/8"ht.
This mug was probably made in the 1880s. The bottom is frosted. It is known only in clear.
Clear $30-35
Ref.- None

588. **HOOK**
1 5/8"dia. x 1 7/8"ht.
This mug is part of a most unusual set. The mug hangs from a glass hook on miniature pitcher. The pitcher has ears that sit on a stand. The stand allows the pitcher to tip and pour without lifting it. The stand is fragile and very easily broken and therefore very rare. This set is known only in clear. A similar pitcher, mug and stand set was made in Tree of Life. The pitcher in the Tree of Life pattern holds 1/2 gallon.
Clear Mug $20-25
Complete Set $400-500
Ref.- GCF1 p. 115, KM6 p. 19, SW1, TOY p. 139

589. **TREE OF LIFE**
2 5/8"dia. x 3 3/8"ht.
This pattern was made by the Boston & Sandwich Glass Co., Hobbs, Brockunier & Co. and the Portland Glass Co. during the 1870s. There is a half gallon pitcher that has a hook on the front from which hangs a mug. The pitcher, also, has "ears" that fit onto a stand. The stand allows the pitcher to tip and pour without lifting it. This set is rare and it is uncertain which manufacturer made it. A similar set was made in Hook, but is miniature. There is also a lemonade (clear and amethyst). The pattern was made primarily in clear, however, some items were made in the scarce colors: amber, light and dark blue, green, cranberry, canary and amethyst. There are over 40 different pieces in the pattern.
Clear Mug $60-70 Clear Set (Mug, Pitcher and Stand) $800-1000
Clear Lemonade $80-100
Amethyst Lemonade $175-200
Ref.- JLPG p. 525

590

591

592

593

594

590. **ZIPPER BAND**
$2\frac{7}{8}$"dia. x $3\frac{1}{2}$"ht.
This souvenired ruby stained mug was probably made about 1900.
Stain $30-35
Ref.- None

591. **BEADED SWAG (HEISEY'S NO. 1295)**
mug: $2\frac{5}{8}$"dia. x $3\frac{1}{4}$"ht. or cup & saucer: $2\frac{3}{4}$"dia. x $1\frac{7}{8}$"ht.
This pattern was manufactured by A. H. Heisey & Co. about 1905. It was produced in clear, green, opalescent, custard and ruby stained. It was a popular souvenir item.
Clear $20-25
Color and Stain $40-55
50% less without saucer
Ref.- HC7 p. 73, MMPG p. 320

592. **ALL OVER STARS**
$2\frac{1}{2}$"dia. x $3\frac{1}{4}$"ht.
This mug was probably manufactured about 1885 by Central Glass Co. It was made in clear, blue and amber.
Clear $20-25
Amber $30-35 Blue $35-40
Ref.- TOY p. 152

593. **SAXON**
$3\frac{1}{8}$"dia. x $3\frac{3}{8}$"ht.
Adams & Co. was the maker of this pattern in the 1880s. After 1891, it was made by the U. S. Glass Co. The mug was produced in clear, opaque white and ruby stain. The ruby stain is often souvenired. Over 70 different items were made in this pattern.
Clear $20-25
Opaque White and Stain $30-35
Ref.- HC5 p. 60 (advertisement), JLPG p. 467, PG&B p. 18 (advertisement), WHPG p. 230

594. **MEPHISTOPHELES, DRAGON HANDLE**
3"dia. x $3\frac{3}{8}$"ht.
This flint mug was probably manufactured in the 1880s. It is probably English or European. The head in a medallion is on both sides. It was made in clear, frosted, opaque white, opaque blue, and transparent brown.
Clear and Frosted $50-60 Opaque White $70-90 Brown & Opaque Blue $100-125
Ref.- AHST p. 221, MMPG p. 368

595

595. **MEPHISTOPHELES, PLAIN HANDLE**
$3\frac{1}{4}$"dia. x $3\frac{1}{4}$"ht.
This mug was probably in the 1880s. It is not known if it's American or European. The head is on both sides. Opaque white is the only color known.
Opaque White $80-100
Ref.- None

597 597

599 598 599

596

600

ART GLASS

These types of glass could be made several different ways. It could be blown, mold blown or pressed.

596. **MARY GREGORY TYPE**
This type glass was probably not decorated by Mary Gregory. It was most likely to have been made in Europe. The glass is usually blown with applied handles. It is decorated with white enameled children or people on a stylized background. In some variations, the hands and face are flesh color. The example shown is an 1893 World's Fair souvenir. This type glass was made in clear, blue, green and cranberry.
Color $100+
Ref.- ART page148 SAN4 page277 (mug not listed)

597. **MOSER TYPE**
The Ludwig Moser factory in Carlsbad, Czechoslovakia is the maker whose name is most often associated with this type of glass. It is known by the quality and amount of decoration on colored glass. Decoration can be heavy gold with enameling or applied transfers. Cups and saucers as well as mugs are known.
All Shapes & Sizes $100+

598. **RUBINA**
The colors in this glass goes from cranberry at the top to clear at the bottom. It is heat sensitive. Handles are applied. These item were often decorated with colored enameling.
All Shapes & Forms $75-100
Ref.- ART page36 (mug not listed)

599. **REVERSE AMBERINA**
Unlike Amberina which goes from red at the top to yellow at the bottom, this glass is yellow at the top and red at the bottom. These items are only known in expanded diamond. The handles are applied.
All Shapes & Forms $75-100

600. **BRISTOL**
Many of these mugs were made in Bristol, England as the name implies, however, many have German writing and were probably made there. Others were probably made in America. This shape and form was produced from about 1860-90. They were only blown and had applied handles. They had a flared lip and a foot. The colors that they were made in include clear, blue, opaque white, opaque blue and opalescent. The decorations included gold, enameled colors and ruby stain. They often had sayings such as "To My Friend" or "Remember Me".
All Color & Decoration $40-90
Ref.- None

601. **AMBERINA**
not shown
The patent for this type of glass was granted to Joseph Locke on July 24, 1883 and assigned to the New England Glass Co. which later became the Libbey Glass Co. This heat sensitive glass was reheated to give its distinctive red coloration at the top which blends to the unheated area at the bottom that is yellow. The design of the form was blown, mold expanded and pressed in a pattern. It was also given decoration by cutting and casing (called plated). Mugs are unusual, but cups are more common.
All Forms $150+
Ref.- ART page17 (mug not listed)

602. **BURMESE**
not shown
Fredrick S. Shirley patented this heat sensitive opaque glass on Dec. 15, 1885. He ran the Mt. Washington Glass Co. The portion of the glass that was reheated is a salmon pink or a muted raspberry and blends into the pale yellow of the rest of the glass. The item of interest is a punch cup or a custard cup and a small mug.
Cup $200-250 Mug $300-350
Ref.- ART page36 (mug not listed)

603. **RUBINA VERDE**
not shown
Hobbs, Brockunier & Co. show a Inverted Thumbprint Rubina Verde mug and a cup in their 1890 catalogue. The colors range from cranberry at the top to vaseline at the bottom. Handles are applied.
All Shapes & Forms $250-350
Ref.- HC3 page67 (advertisement)

604

605

606

607

608

LATER HISTORIC

604. **NIXON-AGNEW ELEPHANT**
3 7/8" dia. x 3" ht.
The Imperial Glass Co. made this blue haze carnival mug for the presidential campaign of 1972. It was also made in blue for 1968. It has eight panels with a picture to represent a different story on each one. This is a remake of the Heisey Elephant mug mold. A collar base was added. The base reads "NIXON, AGNEW and EWR". It also has the Imperial IG trademark. Other varieties of this mug are Nixon-Ford (1976) in black and Ford-Rockefeller (1980) in green.
All Variations $20-25

605. **BICENTENNIAL 2**
3 1/4" dia. x 5 1/4" ht.
This clear stein reads, "E PLURIBUS UNUM 1776-1976" in red and has a gold eagle in a red shield.
Clear $10-15

606. **1984 WORLD EXPOSITION**
2" dia. x 2 7/8" ht.
"84 LOUSIANA WORLD EXPOSITION" is printed on this clear mug with blue lettering. It also says, "MAY 12 TO NOV. 11, 1984".
Clear $10-15

607. **THE 1982 WORLD'S FAIR**
1 1/2" dia. x 1 7/8" ht.
This clear mug is printed with a red flame and black lettering. It says, "THE 1982 WORLD'S FAIR KNOXVILLE, TENNESSEE".
Clear $10-15

608. **LIBERTY BELL TREK**
2 7/8" dia. x 5" ht.
The Liberty Bell is shown on a cart being pulled by horses on this clear stein. Guards are in front and in back of the cart. The design is printed on the glass. The title reads, "PHILADELPHIA TO ALLENTOWN 1777-1977". The stein was made to celebrate the 200th anniversary of moving the bell to prevent its capture.
Clear $10-15

609

609

609. **REPEAL OF PROHIBITION**
2 3/4" dia. x 4 1/4" ht.
The U. S. Glass Co. made this clear mug about 1934 at its Tiffin, Oh. factory. One side shows a man hanging from a tree with the word "PROHIBITION". The other side reads "GOOD BYE FOREVER". Prohibition was repealed Dec. 5, 1933.
Clear $40-45
Ref.- HC5 page178

610. **CINCINNATI BICENTENNIAL (PIG & STYNF)**
3 1/4" dia. x 5" ht.
Anthony D. Gibson Ltd. manufactured this clear mug about 1988. It has a pewter plate signed by the sculptor, Andrew Leicester. He is an Englishman living in Minneapolis, Mn. and has sculptures at the entrance to Sawyer Point Park in that city.
Clear $15-20

611. **CANADA CENTENNIAL**
2 7/8" dia. X 6 1/2" ht.
This white mug is marked "CANADA CENTENNIAL 1867-1967".
White $15-20

612. **BICENTENNIAL**
3 1/4" dia. x 6" ht.
An eagle holding a olive branch in one foot and arrows in the other is shown on this clear stein. It says "1776" above it and "1976" below.
Clear $10-15

613. **MOON WALK**
3" dia. x 3 1/2" ht.
The *Miami Herald* had this mug made to celebrate man landing on the moon.
White & Black $10-15

614. **SAVINGS BONDS**
2 7/8" dia. x 3" ht.
This clear mug was issued to promote the start of the U. S. Savings Bond program in 1939. These bonds were used to help finance Wold War II.
Clear $10-15

615. **MAYFLOWER**
3" dia. x 4" ht.
One side of this clear pressed glass mug shows the ship, Mayflower, with a scroll that says, "1620-1970". The other side of the mug also has a scroll and reads, "6 SEPT 1620" and "CAPE COD 9 NOVEMBER 1620".
Clear $15-20

610

611

612

613

614

615

616

617

618

619

620

616. **STATUE OF LIBERTY**
3" dia. x 6" ht.
The Anchor Hocking Glass Co. made this clear stein about 1989 to celebrate the 100th anniversary and the refurbishing of the Statue of Liberty.
Clear $10-15

617. **CORONATION 1937**
3 1/4" dia. x 3 3/4" ht.
The inscription reads "CORONATION 12 MAY 1937 KING GEORGE VI, QUEEN ELIZABETH". A bust of the king and queen is shown. It was made in amber. Other colors are possible.
Amber $25-30

618. **AGNEW ELEPHANT**
3 1/4" dia. x 4 3/4" ht.
The Imperial Glass Co. made this pink mug about 1970 when Spiro Agnew ran for governor of Maryland. It is a campaign item.
Pink $20-25

619. **NIXON-AGNEW ELEPHANT 2**
3 1/4" dia. x 4 3/4" ht.
The Imperial Glass Co. made this blue mug about 1973 for the presidential campaign
Blue $20-25

620. **AMERICAN FLAG**
2 7/8" dia. x 3 1/4" ht.
This white cased with green mug was probably made about 1918 as a patriotic souvenir of World War I. It has a silver flag, a gold rim and a dark green handle. In silver letters it says, "LONG MAY SHE WAVE".
Green $35-40

621. **EISENHOWER-NIXON**
not shown
3 1/4" dia. x 4 3/4" ht.
The Heisey Glass Co. made this amber mug for the presidential campaign of 1952. It was also made by the Imperial Glass Co.
Color $30-35

622

623

624

625

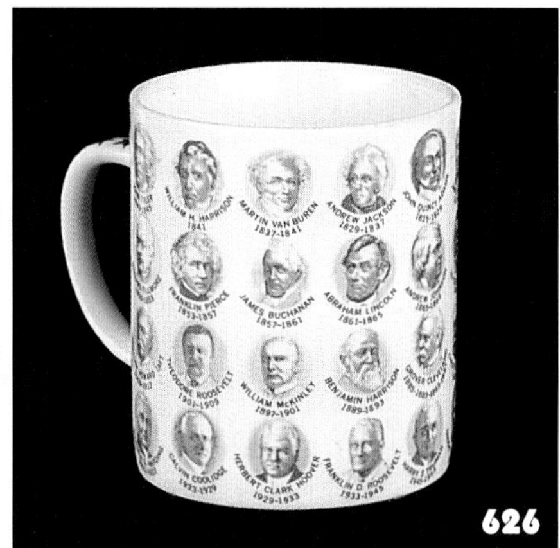

626

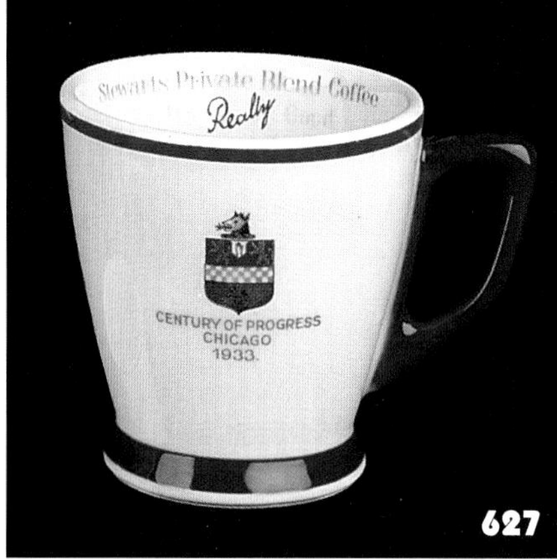

627

628

629

NON-GLASS HISTORIC

622. **THE 1982 WORLD'S FAIR 2**
3 1/8" dia. X 3 1/2" ht.
This white ceramic mug is printed with a red, orange and yellow rainbow. It says, "THE 1982 WORLD'S FAIR KNOXVILLE, TENNESSEE".
Creamic $10-15

623. **GAMES OF THE XXIII OLYMPIAD**
This mug was made to celebrate the 1984 olympics.
Ceramic $10-15

624. **LYNDON B. JOHNSON**
3" dia. x 4 5/8" ht.
This white ceramic mug has a color picture of Johnson on one side, while the other reads "LYNDON B. JOHNSON - 36TH PRESIDENT".
Ceramic $10-15

625. **NIXON-AGNEW 1973**
2 3/4" dia. x 3 3/4" ht.
Frankoma Pottery made this earthenware elephant mug for the 1972 presidential inauguration.
Earthenware $20-25

626. **JIMMY CARTER-PRESIDENT**
3" dia. x 3 1/2" ht.
This white ceramic mug celebrates the 1977 presidential inauguration. It has color photos of each of the presidents with dates in office. It was made in Japan.
Ceramic $10-15

627. **A CENTURY OF PROGRESS**
3 1/2" dia. x 3 1/2" ht.
There is a red ring at the top and a blue ring at the bottom with a blue handle of this white china mug. On the inside of the rim is an advertisement for Stewart's Private Blend Coffee. This was made to celebrate the Chicago World's Fair. The bottom indicates it was made by Baucher China in Weiden, Bavaria.
China $50-60

628. **CORONATION 1953**
2 1/2" dia. x 2 1/2" ht.
This cream colored ceramic mug was issued to celebrate the coronation of Queen Elizabeth II on June 2, 1953. The opposite side has a coat of arms and this date.
Ceramic $10-15

629. **WASHINGTON**
This china mug was made by W. T. Copeland & Son for J. M. Shaw & Co., New York. It has a transfer image of George Washington with flags and an eagle. The other side reads, "A MEMORIAL OF THE CENTENNIAL OF 1876". The mug was sold at a store under the United States Hotel in Philadelphia. The hotel was next to the grounds where the Centennial Exposition was held.
China $150-175
Ref.- CENT page 47 & 73

630. **NIXON-AGNEW 1968**
2 3/4" dia. x 3 3/4" ht.
Frankoma Pottery made this earthenware elephant mug for the 1968 presidential inauguration.
Earthenware $20-25

631. **CARTER-MONDALE**
3" dia. x 4" ht.
Frankoma Pottery made this earthenware donkey mug for the 1977 presidential inauguration.
Earthenware $20-25

632. **GAMES OF THE XXIII OLYMPIAD**
3 3/4" dia. x 3 7/8" ht.
This mug was made in 1980 and given to donors to the Olympic Fund.

633. **NEW YORK WORLD'S FAIR**
3" dia. x 4" ht.
The 1964-65 New York World's Fair is celebrated with this beige ceramic mug with brown lettering.
Ceramic $10-15

634. **MOON LANDING**
3" dia. x 3 1/2" ht.
Crown Royal made this muted white ceramic mug in England to celebrate the first manned moon landing on July 21, 1969. One side shows the lunar landing vehicle, while the other has the names of the astronauts.
Ceramic $10-15

635. **BICENTENNIAL 3**
not shown
3 1/2" dia. x 3 1/2" ht.
The Wilton Brass Co. of Columbia, Pa. hand cast this armetale (resembles pewter) metal mug about 1976. Loren Hancock was the maker. It has an eagle in a medallion.
Metal $10-15

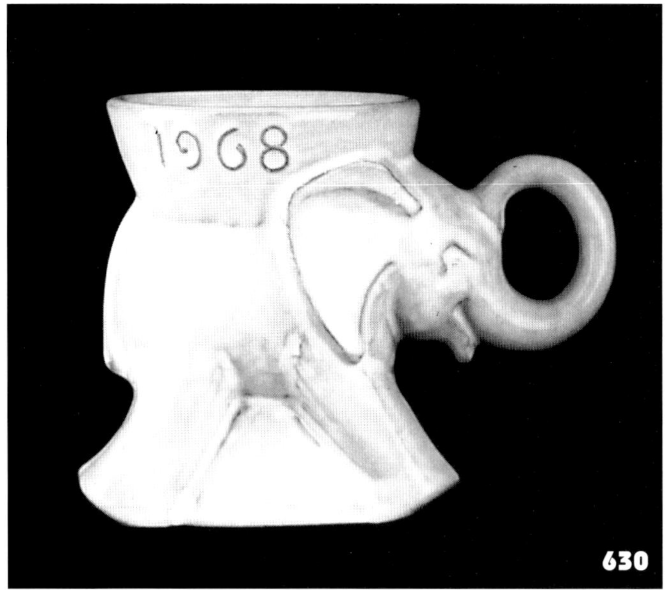

630

631

632

633

634

MUG GROUPS

See page 124
for Group identifications.

Group 1

Group 2

Group 3

Group 4

Group 5

Group 6

Group 7

Group 8

Group 9

Group 10

Group 11

Group 12

Group 13

Group 14

Group 15

Group 16

Group 17

MUG GROUP IDENTIFICATION

Photos shown on pages 120–123.

Group 1.
Deer and Cow
Heron and Peacock
Boy with Begging Dog

Group 2.
BRYCE BEADED HANDLE
Dog Chasing Deer
Bird on a Branch
Pointing Dog
Swan

Group 3.
BRYCE
Chicks and Pugs
Feeding Deer and Dog
Strawberry and Pear
Grape Bunch
Robin in a Tree

Group 4.
TREE OF LIFE WITH SHELL

Group 5.
DOUBLE BEETLE BAND

Group 6.
DEER AND PINETREE

Group 7.
CERES

Group 8.
THOUSAND EYE

Group 9.
SWAN WITH RING HANDLE

Group 10.
OVERSHOT

Group 11.
CUPID AND VENUS

Group 12.
BUTTERFLY SPRAY

Group 13.
BY JINGO

Group 14.
BIRD AND HARP

Group 15.
KNIGHTS OF LABOR

Group 16.
WESTWARD HO

Group 17.
HIGBEE
Rexford
Panelled Thistle
Palm Leaf Fan
Admiral
Colonial, Higbee's
Webb
Arched Fleur-de-Lis

GLASS FACTORIES & THEIR MUGS

** Indicates that attribution to this factory is possible or probable.*

ADAMS & CO.

Alphabet & Children (A.B.C.D.)
Art (Teardrops & Dia. Block)
Atlas (Crystal Ball)
Cottage
Fleur-de-Lis & Drape
Flute
Garfield & Lincoln
Garfield Memorial
Hayes & Wheeler
Hidalgo
Liberty Bell
Paragon (Heavy Panelled Finecut)
Pineapple & Fan
Saxon
Squirrel
Thousand Eye

AETNA GLASS & MANUFACTURING CO.

Hobnail in Square

ATTERBURY & CO.

Robin Atterbury's Eastlake)
Medallion (Ceres)
Leaf (Melon)
Oval and Circle
Peace*
Virtue*
Garfield Shaving Mug
Swan with Ring Handle*
Crossed Cords & Prisms*
Owl ann Horseshoe*
Swimming Swan*
Swimming Swan Variant*
Eastlake (Robin with Wheat)

BAKEWELL, PEARS & CO.

Elongated Double Flute (Ashburton)
Huber
Pitt Diamond (Pitt Honeycomb)
Bakewell Block
Pillar
Thumbprint Stein (Argus)
Flute

A. J. BEATTY & SONS

Beatty Rib
Crested Hobnail
Mitered Block
Beatty Swirl
Good Luck Variant
Spear
Beatty Honeycomb
Hobnail, 7 Rows
Daisy and Button with "V" Orn. (Van Dyke)
Rea (Beaded Swirl)

BEATTY BRADY GLASS CO.

Shrine

BELLAIRE GOBLET CO.

Currier & Ives (Eulalia)
Stars & Bars
Log & Star (Cube and Diamond)
Notched Diamond Rib (Bellaire's # 438)

BELMONT GLASS CO.

Deer & Pinetree*

BOSTON & SANDWICH GLASS CO.

Argus
Fushsia
New England Pineapple
Ashburton
Gooseberry*
Overshot
Beaded Circle
Gothic
Peacock Eye
Bellflower (Ribbed Leaf)
Grape & Festoon with Stip. Leaf
Plain Dodecagon Bottom
Plain Dodecagon Bottom Variant
Bigler
Hairpin (Sandwich Loop)
Prism & Cresent
Bullseye (Lawrence)
Hamilton

BOSTON & SANDWICH GLASS CO.

Prism Panel
Bullseye with Fleur-de-Lis
Hinoto
Ribbed Ivy
Cable
Horn of Plenty
Sandwich Flute
Colonial
Independence Hall*
Tree of Life
Comet
Krom
Union Forever*
Diamond Point

continued next page

continued

Lacy Flower
Waffle
Diamond Thumbprint
(Diamond & Concave)
Worcester
Excelsior
Lacy Heart
Fine Rib
Long Oval with
Bisecting Lines

BRILLIANT GLASS WORKS

Aurora
(Diamond Horseshoe)
Barred Hobnail

BRYCE BROTHERS

Atlas
(Crystal Ball)
Feeding Deer & Dog
Ribbed Forget-Me-Not
(Pert)
Basketweave Variant
Finecut & Panel
Ribbon Candy
Bird on a Branch
Fishscale
(Coral)
Robin in Tree
Block (Red Block, Amber
Block, Clear Block)
Flute
Rosette (Magic)
Carolina (Inverness)
Grape Bunch
Rose in Snow
Cathedral (Orion)
Hobnail
Strawberry & Pear
Chicks & Pugs
Stippled Rose and
Lily of the Valley / In
Fond Rememberance
Swan (Water Fowl)
Curtain (Sultan)
Lousiana
Wheat & Barley
(Duquesne)
Cross Hatching
Panelled Hobnail
Willow Oak (Wreath)
Dog Chasing Deer
Reeded Waffle (Berlin)
Pointing Dog
Brazil (Panelled Daisy)
Stippled Rose &
Lily of the Valley
Curtain (Sultan)

BRYCE, McKEE & CO.

Ashburton with Sawtooth
Bellflower
(Ribbed Leaf)

BRYCE, HIGBEE & CO.

Admiral
(Ribbed Ellipse)
Cut Log (Ethol)
Medallion Sunburst
Arched Fleur-de-Lis
Diamond Point Discs
Three Story (Persian)
Butterfly with Spray (Acme)
Drum
Paris (Zipper Cross)

BRYCE, RICHARDS & CO.

Tulip
Tulip with Sawtooth

BRYCE, WALKER & CO.

Buckle & Star (Orient)
Jacob's Ladder
(Maltese)
Roman Rosette

BURLINGTON GLASS WORKS

Beaded Arch Panels
Dahlia
Swirl Band*
Buckle & Star
Gooseberry*
Three Panel
(R & H's No. 25)*
Thousand Eye*
Daisy & Button with
Crossbar

CAMPBELL, JONES & CO.

Panelled Dewdrop
Rose Sprig

CAMBRIDGE GLASS CO.

Cambridge's No. 2658
Thumbprint on Spearpoint
(Teardrop & Cracked
Ice)
Inverted Strawberry
Divided Block with
Sunburst (Majestic)
Cut Wild Rose

CANTON GLASS CO.

Burred Hobnail
Dahlia
Framed Jewel
Multiple & Scroll
(Canton's No. 130)

CAPE COD GLASS CO.

Hamilton
Hamilton with Leaf
Huber

CENTRAL GLASS CO.

Block (Red Block, Amber
Block, Clear Block)
Centennial Star
Knights of Labor
Cabbage Rose

Cord & Tassel
Oak Leaf Wreath
Centennial Shield
Elephant
Rabbit, Sitting
All Over Stars

CHALLINOR & TAYLOR LTD.
Bird in Nest with Flowers
Kitten
Rabbit, Sitting Variant
Wycliff (Scroll with Star, C&T's No.310)

COLUMBIA GLASS CO.
Basketweave*
Double Beetle Band
Old Columbia (Prism Buttress)
Boy & Girl Face
Double Eye Hobnail with Band
Pointed Jewel
Broken Column
Findlay Hobnail
Raindrop Rings*
Cat on a Cushion (Cat & Dog)
Hobnail
Daisy Band
Long Optic (Tycoon)

CO-OPERATIVE FLINT GLASS CO.
Daisy & Button with Oval Medallion (Pearl)
Panelled Hob
Ivy in Snow (Phoenix's Forest Ware)
Prism Arc (X-Log)*
Lacy Dewdrop

CURLING, ROBERTSON & CO.
Colonial
Flute
Waffle & Thumbprint
Ashburton

DALZELL, GILMORE & LEIGHTON GLASS CO.
Inverted Hobnail Arches
Priscilla (Alexis)
Swirl & Cable
Klondike (Dalzell, G & L's No. 75)
Thumbprint on Spearpoint (Teardrop & Cracked Ice)
Strawberry & Currant (Fruits & Others)

GEORGE DAVIDSON & CO.
Dutch Mill Variant

DIAMOND FLINT GLASS CO.
Dahlia

DIAMOND WARE GLASS CO.
Beaded Shell
Heron
Stork & Rushes Variant*
Vintage Banded*
Fisherman

DITHRIDGE & CO.
Fighting Cats
Monkey & Vines
Picture Frame*
Little Bo-peep
Little Bo-peep Variant
Little Red Riding Hood
Santa & Chimney
Little Buttercup
Owl on a Branch*

DOYLE & CO.
Acanthus Leaves*
Grape & Festoon with Shield
Hobnail with Thumbprint Base
Block (Red Block, Amber Block, Clear Block)
Grape & Festoon with Stip. Leaf
Hobnail with Notched Handle
Doyle's Shell (Cube & Fan)
Hobnail
Triple Triangle
Faceted (Doyle's # 500)

DUNCAN & MILLER GLASS CO.
Blocked Thumbprint Band
Diamond Ridge (Duncan & Miller's No. 48)
Duncan No. 40
Sunburst in Oval (Duncan & Miller's No. 67)
Button Arches

DUGAN GLASS CO.
Fisherman
Stork & Rushes Variant*
Heron
Vintage Banded*
Beaded Shell (New York)

FEDERAL GLASS CO.
Georgia (Peacock Feather)
Penny Candy
Stars & Stripes (Kokomo's # 209)
Kansas
Ribbed Leaves*
Stippled Arrow

continued next page

continued

Panelled Grape
Ribbed Leaves Variant

FENTON ART GLASS CO.
Blackberry Spray*
Orange Tree
Fenton Rose

FINDLAY FLINT GLASS CO.
Stippled Forget-Me-Not

FOSTORIA GLASS CO.
Block (Red Block, Amber Block, Clear Block)
Columbus

GEORGE DUNCAN & SONS
Block (Red Block, Amber Block, Clear Block)
Duncan Block
Grated Diamond & Sunburst (Duncan's No.20)
Duncan's No.904
Tree of Life with Shell*

GEORGE DUNCAN'S SONS
Beaded Swirl
Button Arches
Duncan's No. 40

GILLINDER & SONS
Daisy & Button with Scall. Band
Liberty Bell with Snake
Westmoreland
E Pluribus Unum*
Lion*
Westward Ho
Hobnail
Rustic

GREENSBURG GLASS CO.
Aurora (Diamond Horseshoe)
Sunk Honeycomb (Corona)
Bijou (Fan with Acanthus Leaf)
Barrel Block (Greensburg's No.130)

A. H. HEISEY GLASS CO.
Beaded Swag (Heisey's No. 1295)
Medium Flat Panel
Prince of Wales Plume
Elephant, Heisey's (Fairy Tales)
Kalonyal (Heisey's No. 1776)
Punty Band (Heisey's No. 1220)
Pineapple & Fan, Heisey's (Heisey's No. 1255)
Sunburst in Oval (Heisey's #343 1/2)

J. B. HIGBEE GLASS CO.
Arched Fleur-de-Lis
Lacy Daisy, New Martinsville's
Paris (Zipper Cross)
Arrowhead in Ovals (Madora)
Higbee Ad
Rexford (Alpha)
Colonial, Higbee's (Estelle, Paden City's No. 205)
Palm Leaf Fan
Webb (Paden City's # 203)
Floral Oval
Panelled Thistle (Delta)

HOBBS, BROCKUNIER & CO.
Centennial Star Band
Tree of Life
Viking (Bearded Man)

C. IHMSEN & CO.
Ashburton
Excelsior
Flute

IMPERIAL GLASS CO.
Colonial, Imperial (Imperial's No. 3)
Robin

INDIANA GLASS CO.
Ball & Swirl Variant
Overall Lattice (Indiana's No. 021)
Knurled Dot Band
Shuttle (Heart of Loch Laven)
Paden City
Polka Dot

INDIANA TUMBLER & GOBLET CO.

Austrian
(Finecut Medallion)
Overall Lattice
Shuttle
(Heart of Loch Laven)
Cactus

IOWA CITY GLASS CO.

Begging Dog*
Lamb*
House & Boat Medallion*
Dog with Collar
Lighthouse*

JEFFERSON GLASS CO.

Arrowhead in Ovals
(Madora)
Diamond with Peg
Panelled Thistle*

D. C. JENKINS GLASS CO.

Cherries/Sweetheart
Grapevine with
Thumbprint Band
Panelled Sunflower
Grape/Darling
Panelled Apple
Blossoms/Baby
Panelled Apple
Blossoms/Darling
Strawberry, Falcon
Notched Panels
(Serrated Prism Huber)

KING GLASS CO.

Curled Leaf (Vine Band)
Royal, King's
Vine with Stippling

KING, SONS & CO.

Finecut & Block
Grapevine (Vine)

KOKOMO GLASS CO.

Panelled Cherry/Sweetheart
Stars & Stripes

LaBELLE GLASS CO.

Cord & Tassel

LANCASTER GLASS CO.

Bordered Ellipse
Stippled Cherry

McKEE & BROTHERS

Argus
Diamond Flute
(Flamboyant)
McKinley, Covered
Ashburton
Divided Block with
Sunburst
(Majestic)
McKinley, Protection &
Plenty
Ball & Swirl
Fine Rib
Our Boy / Jester on Pig
Bird & Harp
Grapevine with Ovals
Our Girl / Little Bowpeep
Bryan, Covered
Garden of Eden
(Lotus & Serpent)
Hobnail
Prism
Crystal
Horn of Plenty
Rainbow
Deer & Pinetree
Lutz (Ball & Swirl Variant)
Ray
Excelsior

McKEE GLASS CO.

Bordered Ellipse
Heart Band
Sunk Honeycomb (Corona)
Brittanic
Roman Rosette,
Late (New York)
Troubador
Diamond with Peg

MODEL FLINT GLASS CO.

Block
(Red Block, Amber
Block & Clear Block)
Finecut & Block
Stippled Forget-Me-Not
Deep Star
Star & Ivy*

NATIONAL GLASS CO.

Brittanic
Divided Block with
Sunburst (Majestic)
Serrated Prism
Cactus
Dog & Child
Sunk Honeycomb (Corona)
Cord Drapery
Indoor Drinking Scene
Outdoor Drinking Scene
Troubadour
Deer & Oak Tree
Overall Lattice
Wellsburg
Dewey
Holly (Holly Amber)
Zippered Corners*
Austrian
(Finecut Medallion)
Diamond Spearhead

NEW ENGLAND GLASS CO.

Ashburton

Fine Rib
Waffle & Thumbprint
Bullseye (Lawrence)
Union Forever*
Washington
Bumper to the Flag
New England Pineapple
Diamond Point
Ringed Framed Ovals

NEW MARTINSVILLE GLASS CO.
Lacy Daisy, New Martinsville's
Rexford (Alpha)
Paris (Zipper Cross)
Placid Thumbprint
Polka Dot

H. NORTHWOOD CO.
Dandelion
Stork & Rushes Variant*
Swirl, Northwood's*
Singing Birds
Stump & Vine

NOVA SCOTIA GLASS CO.
Nova Scotia Diamond

NOVELTY GLASS CO.
Columbus

O'HARA GLASS CO.
Cordova
Daisy in Diamond
Hand (Pennsylvania)

PADEN CITY MANUFACTURING CO.
Colonial, Higbee's (Estelle)
Dog & Quail
Webb

PORTLAND GLASS CO.
Dahlia*
Overshot
Roman Rosette*
Finecut & Block*
Panelled Cane (Jewel)*
Tree of Life

RICHARDS & HARTLEY FLINT GLASS CO.
Cupid & Venus
Finecut & Panel
Three Panel
Daisy & Button with Crossbar
Hanover
Two Panel

RIPLEY & CO.
Arched Ovals
Nail
Dakota (Baby Thumbprint)
Pavonia (Pineapple Stem)

RIVERSIDE GLASS WORKS
Box in Box
Petticoat
Brilliant, Riversides

ROBINSON GLASS CO.
Puritan, Robinson's

SPECIALTY GLASS CO.
Bleeding Heart

TARENTUM GLASS CO.
Cane Insert
Heart & Thumbprint
Royal Crystal (Tarentum's Atlanta)
Frost Crystal
Ladder
Tiny Thumbprint
Harvard Yard
Notched Panels

THOMPSON GLASS CO.
Truncated Cube
Torpedo (Pygmy)

UNION GLASS CO.
Bullseye with Fleur-de-Lis
Diamond Thumbprint (Diamond & Concave)
Gothic

U. S. GLASS CO.
Alphabet & Children (A.B.C.D.)
Boy & Girl Face
Cat on a cushion (Cat & Dog)
Duncan Block
Panelled 44 (Athenia)
American Coin (Silver Age)
Brazil (Panelled Daisy)
Electric
Panelled Hobnail
Arched Ovals
Feather Duster
Panelled Palm
Art (Teardrops & Dia. Block)
Feeding Deer & Dog
Pattee Cross
Atlas (Crystal Ball)
Finecut & Panel
Pavonia (Pineapple Stem)
Balder (Pennsylvania)
Fishscale (Coral)
Pointing Dog
Bead & Scroll
Fleur-de-Lis & Drape
Pointed Jewel
Beaded Swirl
Finecut & Panel

Flower with Cane
Portland (Virginia)
Beaded Swirl & Disc
Galloway (Mirror)
Reeded Waffle (Berlin)
Bird on a Branch
Georgia (Peacock Feather)
Ribbed Forget-Me-Not (Pert)
Block (Red Block, Amber Block & Clear Block)
Grape & Festoon with Stippled Leaf
Ribbon Candy
Bohemian (Florodora)
Grape Bunch
Rising Sun
Broken Column
Greek key (U. S. Sheraton)
Robin in Tree
Buckle & Star (Orient)
Hand (Pennsylvania)
Roman Rosette
Bullseye & Fan
Hanover
Royal, King's
Cane Horseshoe
Hidalgo (Frosted Waffle)
Spear
Carolina (Inverness)
Hobnail
Squirrel
Cathedral (Orion)
Kansas (Jewel with Dewdrop)
Star in Bullseye
Chicks & Pugs
Elephant
Kitten
Lacy Daisy
Strawberry & Pear
Colorado (Lacy Medallion)
Loop with Dewdrop
Swan (Water Fowl)
Columbia
Lily of the Valley
Tennessee (Jewel & Cresent)
Columbian Coin
Lousiana
The States (Cane & Star Med.)
Cordova
Old Columbia (Prism Buttress)
Maine (Stippled Panel. Flower)
Thousand Eye
Cottage
Massachusetts
Two Panel
Buckingham (Crosby)
Medallion
Vine with Stippling
Crystal
Michigan (Bulging Loops)
Washington, State Series
Cupid & Venus
Minnesota (Muchness)
Wee Branches
Curled Leaf (Vine Band)
Missouri (Palm & Scroll)
Westmoreland
Daisy & Button with Crossbar
Nail
Willow Oak (Wreath)
Daisy & Button with "V" Ornament
New Hampshire (Bent Buckle)
Wisconsin (Beaded Dewdrop)
Dakota (Baby Thumbprint)
Omnibus (Hobstar)
Wheat & Barley (Duquesne)
Diamond Point Band
Oregon (Beaded Ovals)
Wyoming (Enigma)
Dog Chasing Deer
Panama (Fine Cut Bar)
Swan (Waterfowl)
Strawberry & Pear*

VALLEY GLASS CO.

Monkey with Fancy Handle

WEAR FLINT GLASS WORKS

Diamonds & Prisms Variant
Peabody
Rowing Champion
Gladstone

WESTMORELAND SPECIALTY CO.

Little Bo-Peep, Westmoreland
Capital (Filagree, Estate)
Puritan, Westmoreland's
Shrine, Indian
Eagle Drum
Saint Louis
Star & Lines*
Oriental Penny Candy
Shrine, Fish Handle
Strutting Peacock
Panels
Shrine, Flower
Roman Rosette, Late (New York)

WINDSOR GLASS CO.

Diamond Cut with Leaf (Leaf & Triangle)

Indicates that the manufacturer possibly or probably made this mug or pattern.

GLASS FACTORIES KNOWN TO HAVE MADE MUGS

ADAMS & CO.

Pittsburgh, Pa. 1861-1891

The factory opened as Adams, Macklin & Co. in 1851. They were merged into the U. S. Glass Co. in 1891.

AETNA GLASS & MANUFACTURING CO.

Bellaire, Oh. 1880- 1890

ATTERBURY & CO.

Pittsburgh, Pa. 1865- about 1902

The factory opened as Hale, Atterbury & Co. in 1858.

BAKEWELL, PEARS & CO.

Pittsburgh, Pa. 1836-1883

The factory opened in 1807 as Bakewell & Ensell. In 1809, the company became Bakewell & Co. Then in 1827, the company became Bakewell, Page & Bakewell.

A. J. BEATTY & SONS

Steubenville, Oh. 1845-1889

Tiffin, Oh. 1889-1892

The company was merged into the U. S. Glass Co. in 1892. The Steubenville factory became a warehouse when it's manufacturing equipment was moved to the new Tiffin factory. The Steubenville factory burned in 1903 and was not rebuilt.

BEATTY-BRADY GLASS CO.

Steubenville, Oh. 1895-1898

Dunkirk, In. 1898-1899

The company was merged into the National Glass Co. in 1899.

BELLAIRE GOBLET CO.

Bellaire, Oh. 1876-1888

Findlay, Oh. 1888-1891

The company was purchased by the U. S. Glass Co. in 1891. The factory was closed in 1892.

BELMONT GLASS CO.

Bellaire, Oh. 1866-1890

BOSTON & SANDWICH GLASS CO.

Sandwich, Ma. 1826-1888

The factory started as the Sandwich Manufacturing Co. in 1825. The factory closed because of an unresolved strike. They had difficulty competing with the Midwestern glass houses due to an unwillingness to use soda glass and the availability and expense of raw materials.

BRILLIANT GLASS WORKS

Brilliant, Oh. 1881-1882

The factory burned in 1882 and was rebuilt. The new factory was not successful and was leased to the Dalzell Brothers & Gilmore until 1883 when the company filed bankruptcy. The factory was sold to Gillinder & Sons as a second factory.

BRYCE BROTHERS

Pittsburgh, Pa. 1882-1891

Bryce, Walker & Co. became Bryce Brothers in 1882. They were merged into the U. S. Glass Co. in 1891.

BRYCE, HIGBEE & CO.

Pittsburgh, Pa. 1879-1907

John Bryce, of this company, was the brother of James Bryce, the founder of Bryce, McKee & Co. and had worked for his brothers company. The factory was destroyed by a flood in 1907. A new factory was built and the company was reorganized to become the J. B. Higbee Glass Co. in 1907.

BRYCE, McKEE & CO.

Pittsburgh, Pa. 1850-1854

The company started under this name. It became Bryce, Richards & Co. in 1854.

BRYCE, RICHARDS & CO.

Pittsburgh, Pa. 1854-1965

This factory started as Bryce, McKee & Co. The company became Bryce, Walker & Co. in 1865.

BRYCE, WALKER & CO.

Pittsburgh, Pa. 1865-1882

Bryce, Richards & Co. became Bryce, Walker & Co. in 1865. The company became Bryce Brothers in 1882.

BURLINGTON GLASS WORKS

Burlington, Ont., Can. 1875-1909

CAMBRIDGE GLASS CO.

Cambridge, Oh. 1901-1907

Pittsburgh, Pa. 1907-1957

Their trademark was the words "NEAR CUT" and was added to tableware starting in 1904. A "C" in a triangle was used starting in 1902. The name and molds were acquired by the Imperial Glass Co. in Dec., 1960.

CAMPBELL, JONES & CO.

Pittsburgh, Pa. 1865-1886

Jones, Cavitt & Co. became Campbell, Jones & Co. in 1865. The factory burned in January 1891, but was rebuilt. It closed in 1895.

CANTON GLASS CO.

Canton, Oh. 1883-1899

The company was merged into the National Glass Co. in 1899.

CENTRAL GLASS CO.

Wheeling, W. V. 1863-1891

The company merged into the U. S. Glass Co. in 1891. A labor dispute closed the factory in 1893. In 1896, a new factory was started using the old name in Summitville, In. and was in business until 1939.

CHALLINOR & TAYLOR CO. LTD.

Pittsburgh, Pa. 1866-1884

Tarentum, Pa. 1884-1893

The original company started in Pittsburgh as the Challinor, Hogan Glass Co. The company joined the U. S. Glass Co. in 1891. The factory burned and was never rebuilt shortly after the merger.

COLUMBIA GLASS CO.

Findlay, Oh. 1886-1891

The company merged into the U. S. Glass Co. in 1891. The factory was closed due to a strike in 1893 and never reopened.

CO-OPERATIVE FLINT GLASS CO.

Beaver Falls, Pa. 1889-1937

The factory started as the Beaver Falls Co-Operative Glass Co. in 1879. In 1937, some of the molds were acquired by the Phoenix Glass Co. to settle a debt.

CURLING, ROBERTSON & CO.

Pittsburgh, Pa. 1834-1860

The company started as The Fort Pitt Glass Works in 1827. The next year it became R. B. Curling & Co. when William Price left and Curling's two sons joined the company. Morgan Robertson joined the company in 1834. The company became Dithridge & Co. in 1860.

DALZELL, GILMORE & LEIGHTON GLASS CO.

Findlay, Oh. 1888-1898

They started business as the Dalzell Brothers & Gilmore in 1883. They were merged into the National Glass Co. in 1899. The factory closed in 1902.

GEORGE DAVIDSON & CO.

England 1867-1957

This company's trademark was a lion on turret of a castle. They became the Brama Works in 1957.

DIAMOND FLINT GLASS CO.

Montreal, Quebec, Can. 1903-1913

DIAMOND GLASS-WARE CO.

Indiana, Pa. 1913-1931

The factory burned in 1931 and was never reopened.

DITHRIDGE & CO.

Pittsburgh, Pa. 1860-1881

Martins Ferry, Oh. 1881-1887

They started as the R. B. Curling Co. in 1850.

DOYLE & CO.

Pittsburgh, Pa. 1861-1891

The company merged into the U. S. Glass Co. in 1891. The factory was closed by the strike of 1903 and never reopened.

DUNCAN & MILLER GLASS CO.

Pittsburgh, Pa. 1894-1955

DUGAN GLASS CO.

Indiana, Pa. 1904-1913.

Their trademark, c. 1907, was a "D" in a diamond. The company became the Diamond Glass-Ware Co. in 1913.

FEDERAL GLASS CO.

Columbus, Oh. 1901-1978

Production usage of their "F" in a shield trademark began in 1932.

FENTON ART GLASS CO.

Williamstown, W. V. 1906- present

Frank L. Fenton's brother, John, left the company in 1908 to form the Millersburg Glass Co., but that company only lasted until 1912.

FINDLAY FLINT GLASS CO.

Findlay, Oh. 1888-1891

The factory was destroyed by fire in June 1891 and was never rebuilt.

FOSTORIA GLASS CO.

Fostoria, Oh. 1887-1892

Moundsville, W. V. 1892- 1986

GEORGE DUNCAN & SONS

Pittsburgh, Pa. 1881-1886

This company started as George Duncan in 1874. It became George Duncan's Sons in 1886.

GEORGE DUNCAN'S SONS

Washington, Pa. 1886-1891

This company was merged into the U. S. Glass Co. in 1891. The factory was closed by the strike of 1893 and never reopened. The sons, A. H. Heisey (son-in-law) and George Duncan Jr. became officers in the U. S. Glass Co., but were soon disillusioned and left. They went West to seek their fortunes. They returned to form the Duncan & Miller Glass Co. and the A. H. Heisey Glass Co. in 1894 and 1895 respectively.

GILLINDER & SONS

Pittsburgh, Pa. 1867-1891

This company started business as the Franklin Flint Glass Co. in 1861. In 1863, it became Gillinder & Bennet. In 1867, Bennet left the business and William Gillinder's sons, Fredrick and James, entered the business. The company sold to the U. S. Glass Co. in 1891. Part of the terms for the sale were they couldn't manufacture glass for 20 years. The factory was closed by the strike of 1903 and never reopened. Gillinder Brothers was started in 1912.

GREENSBURG GLASS CO.

Greensburg, Pa. 1889-1899

The company merged into the National Glass Co. in 1899.

A. H. HEISEY GLASS CO.

Newark, Oh. 1895-1958

Their trademark was an "H" in a diamond and usage started in 1900. When the factory closed, the Imperial Glass Co. purchased some of the pattern molds and names. They did not remove the trademark when making these items.

JOHN B. HIGBEE GLASS CO.

Bridgeville, Pa. 1907-1915

This company started as Bryce, Higbee & Co. in 1879. Occasionally, pattern items made by this company will have a trademark. It is a bee with the letter "H, I & G" across the wings and body. Some of the pattern glass molds were sold to the New Martinsville Glass Manufacturing Co. and the Paden City Glass Manufacturing Co. It appears that these companies did not remove the bee trademark.

HOBBS, BROCKUNIER & CO.

Wheeling, W. V. 1863-1891

They started business as Hobbs, Barnes & Co. The name was changed after Barnes and his son had died. The company merged into the U. S. Glass Co. in 1891. The company shut down during the strike of 1893 and never re-opened, although the plant was renovated and operated as the H. Northwood Co. from 1902 to 1925.

C. IHMSEN & CO.

Pittsburgh, Pa. about 1855

This company started as C. Ihmsen before 1850.

IMPERIAL GLASS CO.

Bellaire, Oh. 1904-1984

The company started using the "NUCUT" trademark in 1911, the 1913 trademark had letters "IM,PE,RI&AL" in each corner of a cross and the 1951 trademark had the letters "I and G" superimposed.

INDIANA GLASS CO.

Dunkirk, In. 1897-1899 restart 1908-present

The company merged into the National Glass Co. in 1899.

INDIANA TUMBLER & GOBLET CO.

Greentown, In. 1894-1899

The company merged into the National Glass Co. in 1899. The factory closed after a fire in 1903.

IOWA CITY GLASS CO.

Iowa City, Ia. 1880-1882

JEFFERSON GLASS CO.

Steubenville, Oh. 1901-1907

Follansbee, Oh. 1907-1913

Toronto, Can. 1913-1935

After 1920, they primarily produced lighting fixtures. Some pieces are marked with their trademark, "Krys-Tol".

D. C. JENKINS GLASS CO.

Kokomo, In. 1906-1932

This company started as the Kokomo Glass Glass Co. in 1900.

KING GLASS CO.

Pittsburgh, Pa. 1880-1891

The company merged into the U. S. Glass Co. in 1891. The strike of 1893, which involved all of the U. S. Glass Co. factories, started at this factory.

KING, SONS & CO.

Pittsburgh, Pa. 1869-1880

This company started as the Cascade Glass Co. In 1864, the company became Johnson, King & Co. The company became the King Glass Co. in 1880.

KOKOMO GLASS CO.

Kokomo, In. 1900-1905

The factory was destroyed by fire in 1905. When it was rebuilt in 1906, it became the D. C. Jenkins Glass Co.

LaBELLE GLASS CO.

Bridgeport, Oh. 1872-1888

The factory closed Apr. 2, 1888. A fire that almost destroyed the factory the year before is blamed for causing the finances of the company collapse. The factory sold and became the Muhleman Glass Works

LANCASTER GLASS CO.

Lancaster, Oh. 1908-1937

The company was merged into the Hocking Glass Co.

McKEE & BROTHER

Pittsburgh, Pa. 1865-1889

Jeannette, Pa. 1889-1899

The company originated as McKee & Brother in 1853. The company merged into the National Glass Co. in 1899. The factory left National in 1903 to become the McKee Glass Co.

McKEE GLASS CO.

Jeannette, Pa. 1903-1951

McKee & Brothers left the National Glass Co. in 1903 to become the McKee Glass Co.

Their trade mark was "Pres-Cut" from 1903 to 1904. After 1904, their trademark became "American Pres-Cut Glass" in a circle. In 1951, the company was purchased by the Thatcher Glass Manufacturing Co. The factory is now the Jeannette Glass Co.

MODEL FLINT GLASS CO.

Findlay, Oh. 1888-1894

Albany, In. 1894-1899

The company merged into the National Glass Co. in 1899. The factory closed in 1902.

NATIONAL GLASS CO.

1899-1904

The factories were:

Beatty-Brady Glass Co.
McKee & Brothers
Model Flint Glass Co.
Central Glass Co. - Summitville, In.
H. Northwood Glass Co.
Crystal Glass Co.
Ohio Flint Glass Co.
Cumberland Glass Co.
Riverside Glass Co.
Dalzell, Gilmore & Leighton Co.
Robinson Glass Co.
Fairmont Glass Co.
Rochester Tumbler Co.
Greensburg Glass Co.
Royal Glass Co.
Indiana Tumbler & Goblet Co.
West Virginia Glass Co.
Keystone Tumbler Co.

The Canton Glass Co. joined the merger soon after it was formed. By 1904, some factories closed, others left the merger to resume business on their own, some were dismantled, and others were leased or sold.

NEW ENGLAND GLASS CO.

Cambridge, Ma. 1817-1888

They became the W. L. Libbey & Sons Glass Co. in 1888 and moved to Toledo, Oh. The company is still in business today and is known as The Libbey Glass Co.

NEW MARTINSVILLE GLASS MANUFACTURING CO.

New Martinsville, W. V. 1900-1944

The company's assets were used to start the Viking Glass Co. in 1944.

H. NORTHWOOD GLASS CO.

Martins Ferry, Oh. 1888-1892
Ellwood City, Pa. 1892-1896
Indiana, Pa. 1896-1903
Wheeling, W. V. 1902-1925

The underlined "N" in a circle trademark was introduced about 1906.

NOVA SCOTIA GLASS CO.

Trenton, Nova Scotia, Canada 1881-1892

This company was also called the Diamond Glass Co.

NOVELTY GLASS CO.

Fostoria, Oh. 1891-1892

The company was sold to the U. S. Glass Co. in 1892. The factory burned in 1893 and was not rebuilt.

O'HARA GLASS CO.

Pittsburgh, Pa. 1875-1891

The company started as James B. Lyon & Co. in 1848. The company merged into the U. S. Glass Co. in 1891. The factory was closed during the strike of 1893 and never re-opened.

PADEN CITY MANUFACTURING CO.

Paden City, W. V. 1916-1951

PIONEER GLASS CO. LIMITED

Pittsburgh, Pa. 1891- ?

They were primarily a ruby stain decorating company.

PORTLAND GLASS CO.

Portland, Me. 1864-1873

The factory was destroyed by fire in 1867, but it was soon in operation again. The economic condition of the company worsened until it was necessary to re-organize in 1870. However, conditions did not improved and the factory closed in 1873. There is no larger controversy in glass collecting than which patterns were made by this company.

RICHARDS & HARTLEY FLINT GLASS CO.

Tarenum, Pa. 1866-1891

This company merged into the U. S. Glass Co. in 1891. The factory was sold to the Tarenum Glass Co. in 1894.

RIPLEY & CO.

Pittsburgh, Pa. 1866-1891

The company was merged into the U. S. Glass Co. in 1891. The factory closed about 1902.

RIVERSIDE GLASS WORKS

Wellsburg, W. V. 1879-1900 1903-1907

The company merged into the National Glass Co. in 1900. The factory was leased to a holding company as the Riverside Glass Co. by the National Glass Co. from 1903-1907. In 1907, it was sold to the Crescent Glass Co. which stayed in business until 1982.

ROBINSON GLASS CO.

Zanesville, Oh. 1893-1900

They merged into the National Glass Co. in 1900 and quickly closed.

SPECIALTY GLASS CO.

Grapeville, Pa. 1889-1892

The company became the Westmoreland Specialty Co. in the 1892.

THOMPSON GLASS CO. LTD.

Uniontown, Pa. 1899-1892

TARENTUM GLASS CO.

Tarentum, Pa. 1866-1918

The factory burned in 1918 and was not reopened.

UNION GLASS CO.

Sommerville, Ma. 1851-1924

The company failed in 1860, but was quickly reorganized.

U. S. GLASS CO.

1891-1963

The following factories merged to form the U. S. Glass Co.:

Adams & Co.	Factory "A"
Bellaire Goblet Co.	Factory "M"
Bryce Brothers	Factory "B"
Central Glass Co.	Factory "O"
Challinor & Taylor Ltd.	Factory "C"
Columbia Glass Co.	Factory "J"
Doyle & Co.	Factory "P"
George Duncan's Sons	Factory "D"
Gillinder & Sons	Factory "G"
Hobbs, Brockunier & Co.	Factory "H"
King Glass Co.	Factory "K"
Nickel Plate Glass Co. Fostoria, Oh.	Factory "N"
O'Hara Glass Co.	Factory "L"
Richards & Hartley Flint Glass Co.	Factory "E"
Ripley & Co.	Factory "F"

A. J. Beatty & Sons, a factory at Gas City and the Novelty Glass Co. were added in 1892 and factory "U" was added at Glassport in 1894. A strike from 1893-1896 caused the closing of all but a handful of these factories. They were Factories: "A" (Adams & Co.), "R" (A. J. Beatty & Sons - Tiffin), "B" (Bryce Brothers), "K" (King), "E" (Richards & Hartley Flint Glass Co.), and "F" (Ripley & Co.). 4 more factories were added about 1910. These were: Factory "D" (gold decorating), Factory "H" (plate etching), Factory "N" (decorating) and Factory "O" (tank operation). The trademark, "U. S.", was used after 1914. Many of the factories closed during the great depression in the 1930s. Only the Glassport and the Tiffin factories remained in 1963. The Glassport factory was destroyed by a tornado that year and the Tiffin factory became the Tiffin Art Glass Co. That factory closed in 1985.

VALLEY GLASS CO.

Beaver Falls, Pa. 1890-1892

This company was started as the Whitla Glass Co. in 1887. The factory burned in 1892 and was never rebuilt.

WEAR FLINT GLASS WORKS

Sunderland, Eng. 1858-present

The company was also called Henry Greener & Co. during the middle years of its history. In 1878, they began using their lion holding a star trademark.

WESTMORELAND SPECIALTY CO.

Grapeville, Pa. early 1892-1923

This company started as the Specialty Glass Co. about 1889. The factory was located in East Liverpool, Oh. and later moved to Grapeville, Pa. In 1923, the company became the Westmoreland Glass Co. and was in business until 1985.

WINDSOR GLASS CO.

Pittsburgh, Pa. about 1886 - about 1895

The factory was burned in 1887, but was soon rebuilt.

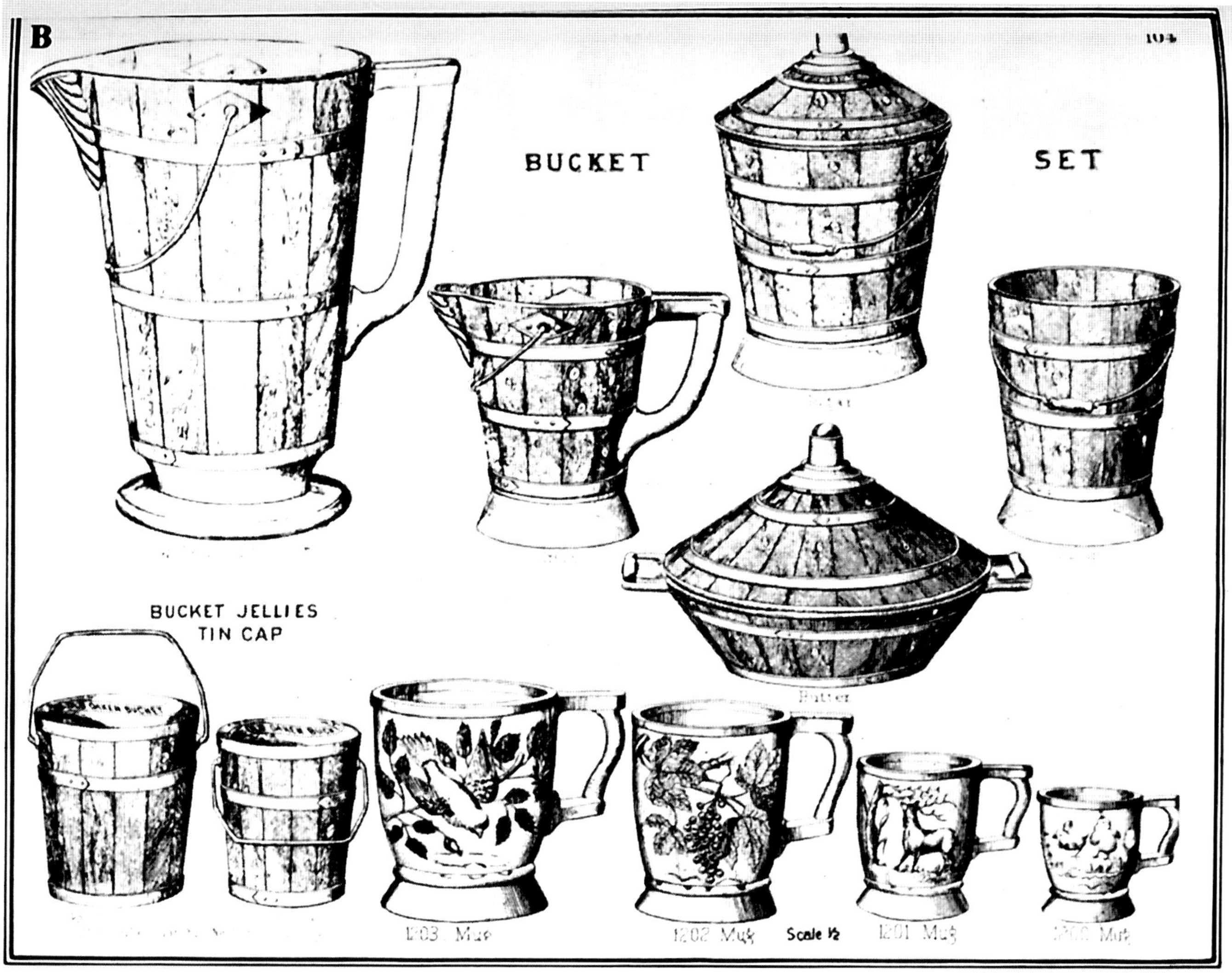

B

104

BUCKET SET

BUCKET JELLIES
TIN CAP

1203 Mug

1202 Mug Scale ½

1201 Mug

1200 Mug

(HC5 p.81)

Strawberry & Pug, Grape Bunch, Feeding Deer & Dog, Chicks & Pugs.

(HC5 p.63)

Cottage.

(<u>HC5</u> p.86) **Swan, Pointing Dog, Bird on a Branch, Dog Chasing Deer.**

(<u>HC5</u> p.131)
Pointed Jewel.

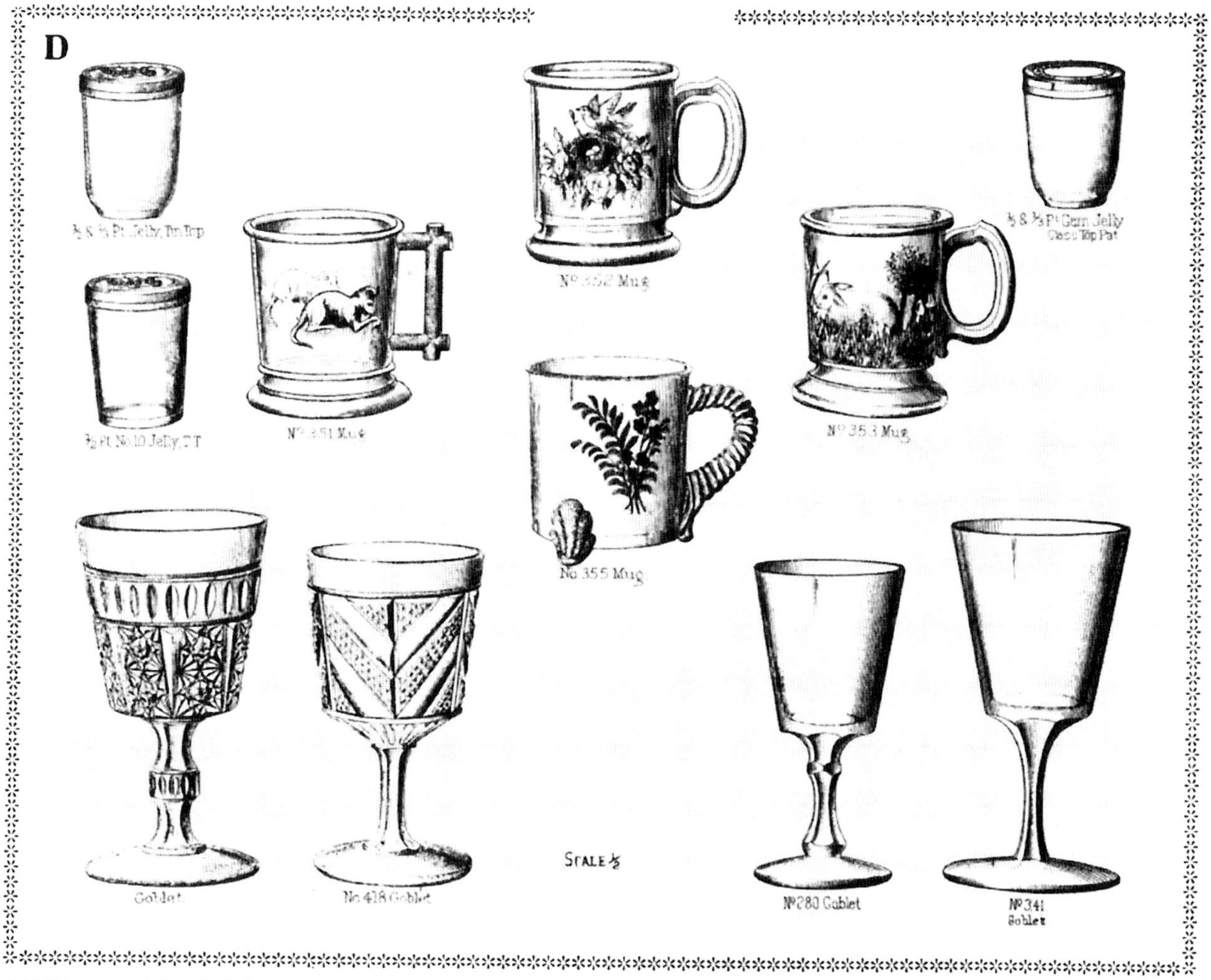

D
½ & ⅓ Pt. Jelly, Tin Top
½ & ⅓ Pt Gem Jelly
Glass Top Pat
⅓ Pt No.10 Jelly, T.T
No. 351 Mug
No. 352 Mug
No. 353 Mug
No. 355 Mug
Goblet
No. 418 Goblet
SCALE ½
No. 280 Goblet
No. 341
Goblet

(HC5 p.91) **Rabbit Sitting, Kitten, Bird in Nest with Flowers.**

A
No. 25
WARE.
25 Sugar & Cov
SETT.
25 Butter & Cov

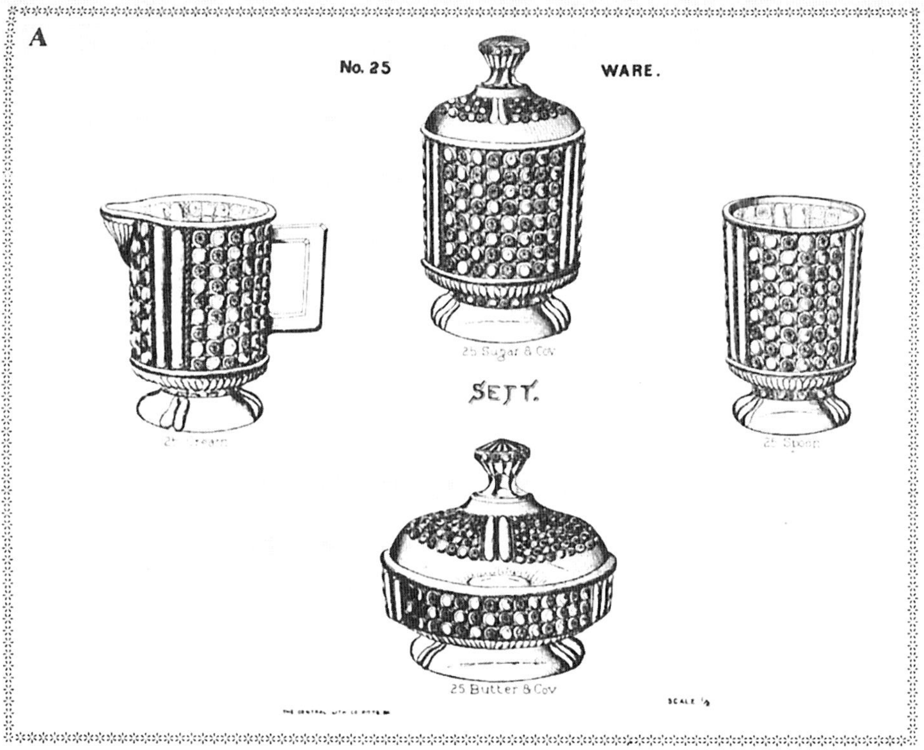

(HC5 p.113) **Three-Panel.**

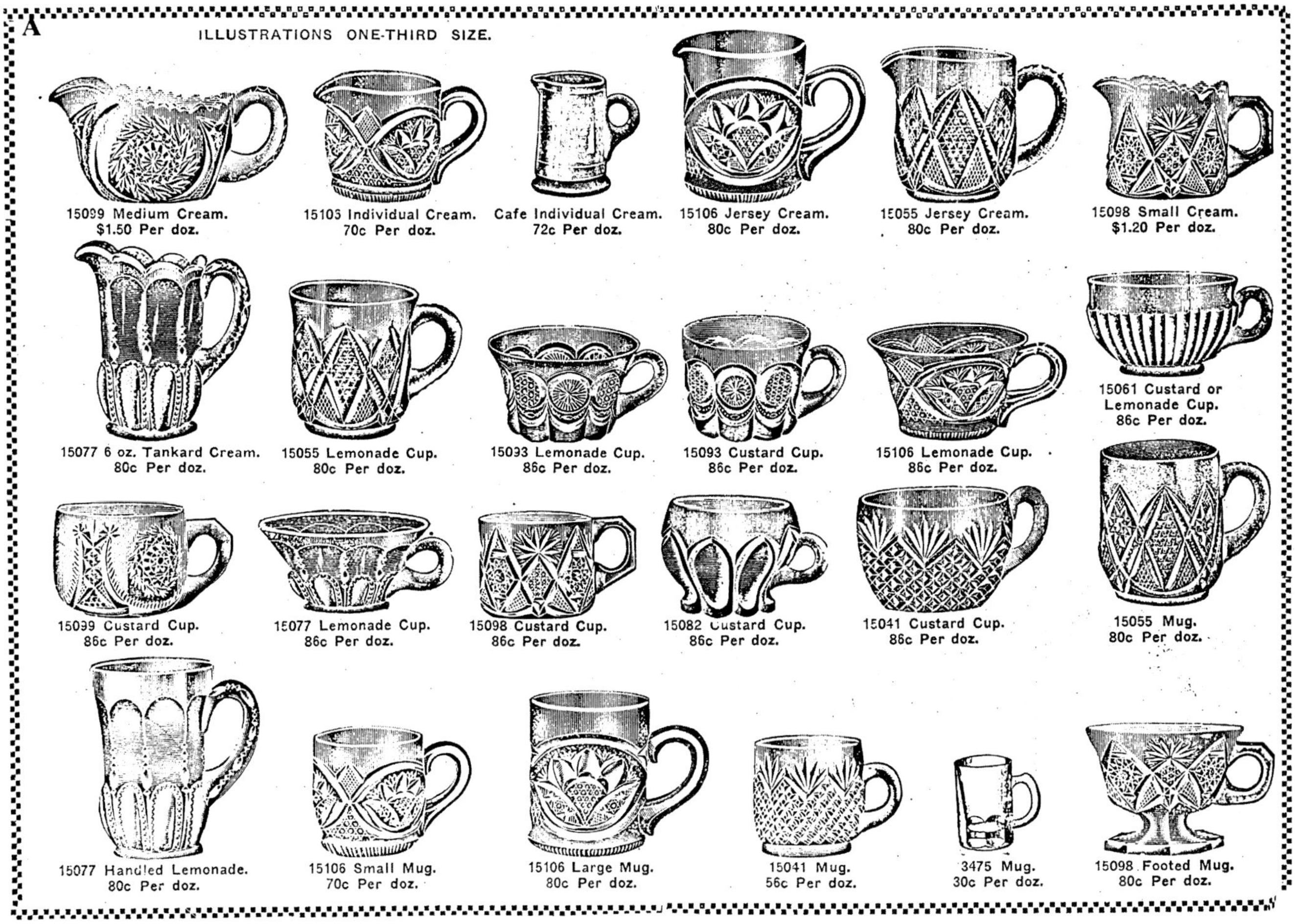
A
ILLUSTRATIONS ONE-THIRD SIZE.
15099 Medium Cream. $1.50 Per doz.
15103 Individual Cream. 70c Per doz.
Cafe Individual Cream. 72c Per doz.
15106 Jersey Cream. 80c Per doz.
15055 Jersey Cream. 80c Per doz.
15098 Small Cream. $1.20 Per doz.
15077 6 oz. Tankard Cream. 80c Per doz.
15055 Lemonade Cup. 80c Per doz.
15093 Lemonade Cup. 86c Per doz.
15093 Custard Cup. 86c Per doz.
15106 Lemonade Cup. 86c Per doz.
15061 Custard or Lemonade Cup. 86c Per doz.
15099 Custard Cup. 86c Per doz.
15077 Lemonade Cup. 86c Per doz.
15098 Custard Cup. 86c Per doz.
15082 Custard Cup. 86c Per doz.
15041 Custard Cup. 86c Per doz.
15055 Mug. 80c Per doz.
15077 Handled Lemonade. 80c Per doz.
15106 Small Mug. 70c Per doz.
15106 Large Mug. 80c Per doz.
15041 Mug. 56c Per doz.
3475 Mug. 30c Per doz.
15098 Footed Mug. 80c Per doz.

(HC5 p.152)
Buckingham, Pineapple & Fan, Minnesota, The States, Columbia, Michigan.

(HC5 p.112)
Daisy & Button "V" & "X" Bar.

B
MADE IN CRYSTAL, AMBER, BLUE, & CANARY.
31
"MIKADO"
NO 99 PATTERN

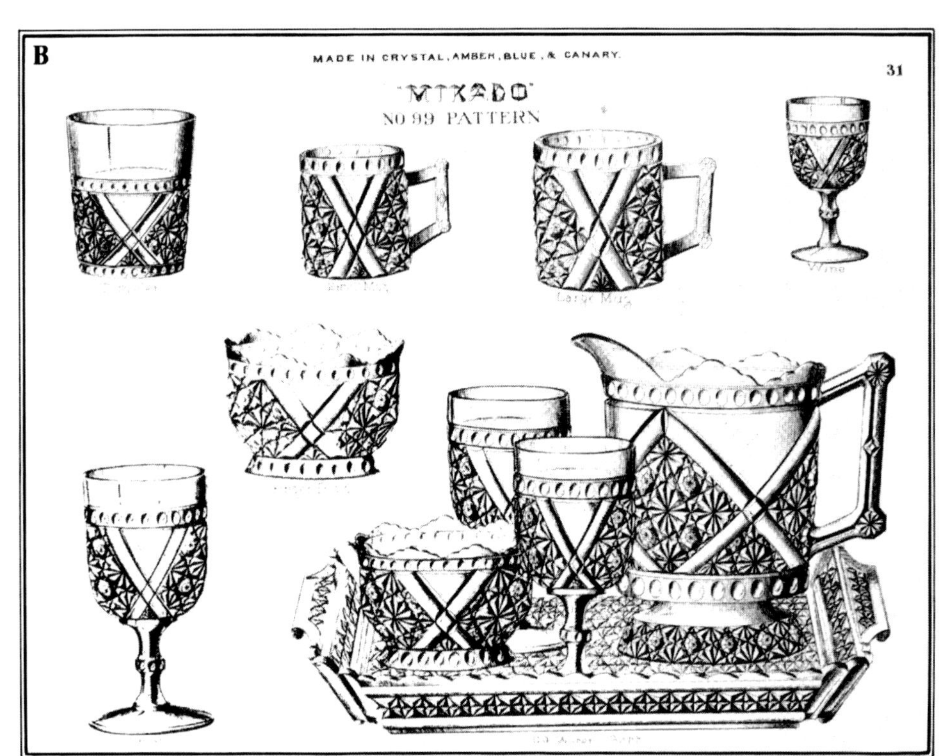

12 CHINA, GLASS AND LAMPS.

McKEE & BROTHERS,

PITTSBURGH, PA.

9 in. McKinley Plate; also, Etched Head; also, Gold Ground.

McKinley Handled Mug. 8 oz.

7 in. McKinley Plate; also, Etched Head; also, Gold Ground.

SCALE, HALF SIZE.

We also furnish tumblers with McKinley head pressed in bottom. Also, with McKinley or Hobart profile etched on side.

SALESMEN.

NEW YORK—66 West Broadway.
SAN FRANCISCO—310 Front Street.
EAST—{ E. W. Nickerson. J. A. Harris.

WEST—{ Thos. H. Lohr. Frank M. Miller.
SOUTH—{ A. J. George. H. E. Waddell.

(HC0 p.96) **McKinley "Protection & Plenty".**

(HC5 p.85) **Buckle & Star.**

(HC5 p.147) **Tennessee.**

(HC6 p.80) **Button Arches.**

(HC5 p.149) **Colorado.**

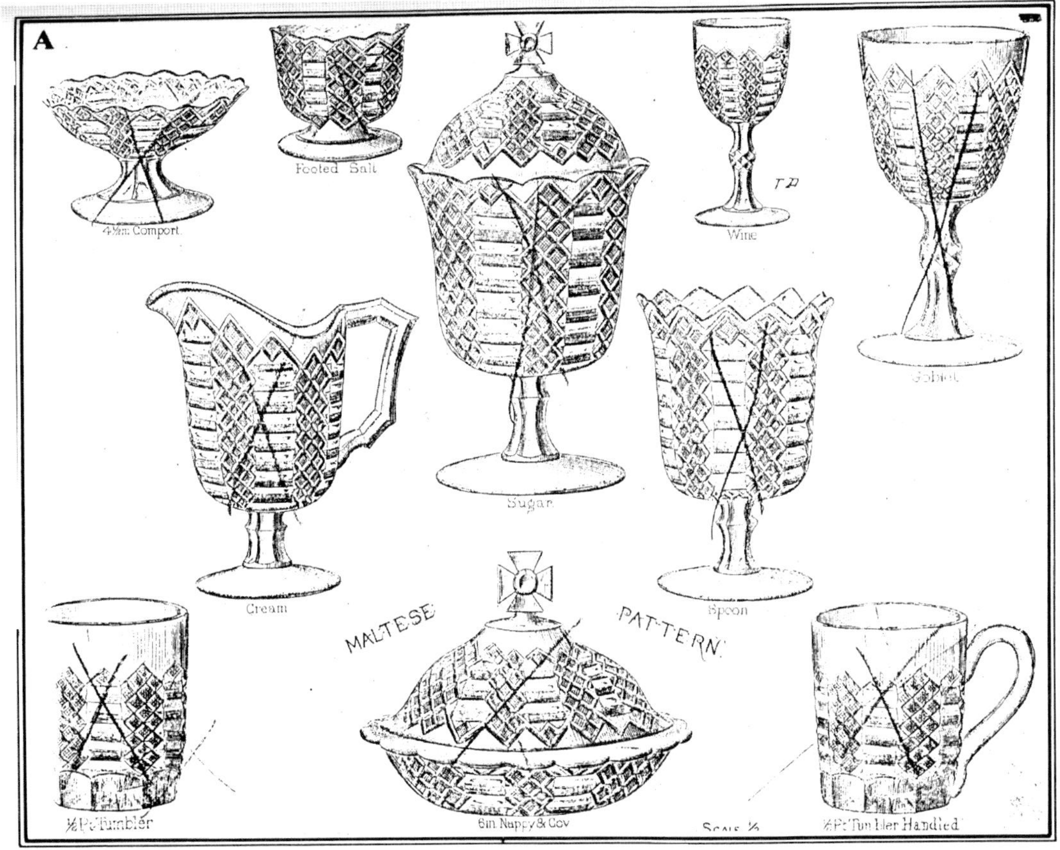

(HC5 p.85) **Jacobs Ladder.**

PATTERN PICTURES: MUG NOT SHOWN

Art

Atlas

Bakewell Block

Belted Worchester

Bigler

Britanic

Bullseye with Fleur-de-Lis

Cable

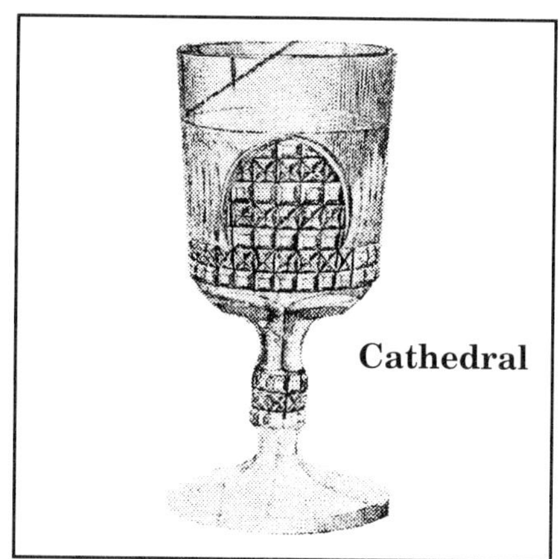
Cathedral

Comet

Diamond Quilted

Electric

Feather Duster

Fine Cut and Block

Frost Crystal

Grape & Festoon with Stippled Leaf

Hamilton with Leaf

Inverted Strawberry

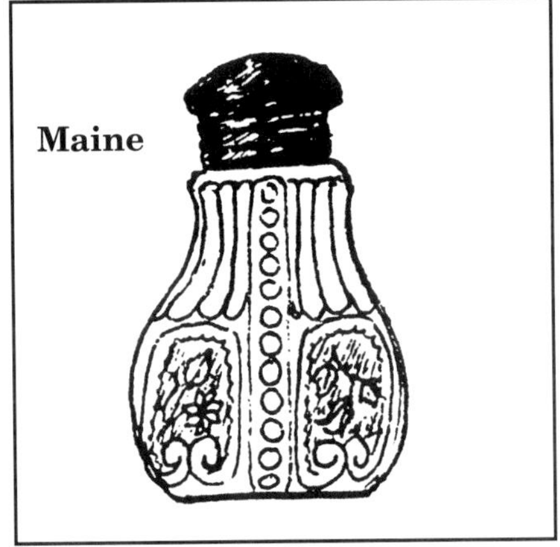
Maine

Medallion

New England Pineapple

O'Hara Diamond

Ribbon Candy

Rosette

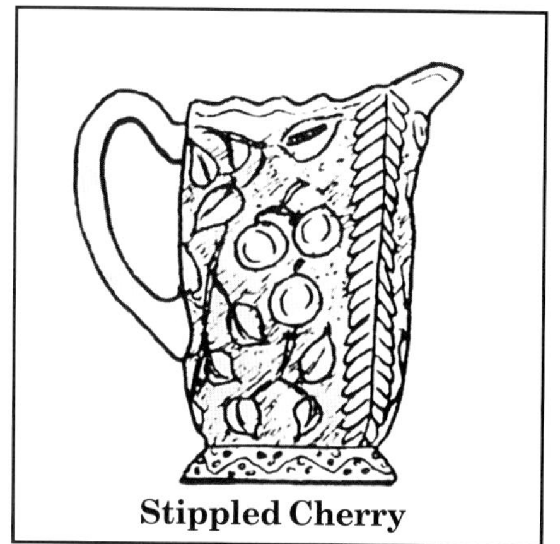
Stippled Cherry

Tulip with Sawtooth

Two Panel

Victoria Pioneer's

Waffle with Thumbprint

Washington

Westmoreland

BIBLIOGRAPHY

ALB *The Beauty of Albany Glass* by Marcelle Bond

AG *American Glass* by George S. and Hellen McKearin

AHST *American Historical Glass* by Bessie Lindsey

ART *19th Century Art Glass* by A. C. Revi

AS *American Story Recorded in Glass* by Tracy Marsh

BAKE *Bakewell, Pears & Co. catalogue from about 1875*

CAM1 *Cambridge Glass Catalogue 1903*

CAM2 *Cambridge Glass Catalogue 1910*

CARN *Std. Encyclopedia of Carnival Glass* by Bill Edwards

CENT *The 1876 Centennial Collectables & Price Guide* by Stan Gores

CLUB *The Glass Club Bulletin - National Early American Glass Club Winter, 1986/87 American Glass,at American Fairs - Some New Discoveries* by Jane Shadel Spillman

COOP *Co-Operative Flint Glass Catalogue*

CORN *American Pressed Glass in the Corning Museum of Glass* by Jane Shadel Spillman

DAZ *Depression Glass Daze - March 1, 1983* front p.

ENG *English Pressed Glass 1830-1900* by Raymond Slack

ENGP *English 19th Century Press - Moulded Glass* by Colin Lattimore

FIN *Findlay Glass* by James Measell and Don Smith

FINP *Findlay Pattern Glass* by Don Smith

FOS *A History of Fostoria, Ohio Glass* by Melvin Murray

GCD1 *Glass Collector's Digest - Apr. / May 1989 "Assorted Color Mugs"* by G. Eason Eige

GCD2 *Glass Collector's Digest June-July 1994 "Milk Glass - Arsenic & Lacy Edge Plates"* by G. Eason Eige

GCF1 *Children's Glass Dishes, China & Furniture Vol.1* by Doris A. Lechler

GCF2 *Children's Glass Dishes, China & Furniture Vol.2* by Doris A. Lechler

GOB1 *American & Canadian GobletsI* by Doris and Peter Unitt

GOB2 *American & Canadian GobletsII* by Doris and Peter Unitt

GR1 *Glass Review - June, 1980* p. 20

GR2 *Glass Review - June, 1982* p. 6

GR3 *Glass Review - Oct., 1982* p. 10

GRE *Greentown Glass* by James Measell

GREE *Greentown Glass* by Ruth Herrick

HC2 *Book 2 - Opalescent Glass from A-Z* by William Heacock

HC4 *Book 4 - Custard Glass* by William Heacock

HC5 *Book 5 - U. S. Glass from A-Z* by William Heacock

HC6 *Book 6 - Oil Cruets from A-Z* by William Heacock

HC7 *Book 7 - Ruby Stained Glass from A-Z* by William Heacock

HCG1 *Collecting Glass - Vol. 1* by William Heacock

HCG2 *Collecting Glass - Vol.2* by William Heacock

HCG3 *Collecting Glass - Vol. 3* by William Heacock

HCO *Old Pattern Glass According to Heacock* by William Heacock

HCP1 *Pattern Glass Preview, Issue #1* by William Heacock

HCP2 *Pattern Glass Preview, Issue #2* by William Heacock

HCP3 *Pattern Glass Preview, Issue #3* by William Heacock

HCP6 *Pattern Glass Preview, Issue #6* by William Heacock

HCT *1,000 Toothpick Holders* by William Heacock

HGC1 *The Glass Collector, ssue #1* article by William Heacock

HGC2 *The Glass Collector, Issue #2* article by William Heacock

HGC4 *The Glass Collector, Issue #4* article by William Heacock

HGC5 *The Glass Collector, Issue #5* article by William Heacock

HOB1 *Hobbies Magazine- Apr., 1949 "Toy Mugs - A Fresh & Interesting Field for Collecting"*

HOB2 *Hobbies Magazine- May 1973 an article* by Mary and Bill Wolletts

HOB3 *Hobbies Magazine- June1973 an article* by Mary and Bill Wolletts

HOB4 *Hobbies Magazine- Nov., 1973 an article* by Mary and Bill Wolletts

HOB5 *Hobbies Magazine- June, 1974 an article* by Mary and Bill Wolletts

HSY *Heisey's Glassware of Distinction* by Mary Louise Burns

IOW *Iowa City Glass* by Miriam Richter

JJ *Just Jenkins* by Joyce Hicks

JLPG *Early American Pattern Glass 1850-1910* by Bill Jenks and Jerry Luna

KM3 *A Third Pitcher Book* by Minnie Watson Kamm

KM5 *A Fifth Pitcher Book* by Minnie Watson Kamm

KM6 *A Sixth Pitcher Book* by Minnie Watson Kamm

KM7 *A Seventh Pitcher Book* by Minnie Watson Kamm

KM8 *An Eighth Pitcher Book* by Minnie Watson Kamm

LEE *Early American Pattern Glass* by Ruth Webb Lee

LEEV *Victorian Glass* by Ruth Webb Lee

MET1 *Early American Pattern Glass* by Alice Huelett Metz

MET2 *Much More Early American Pressed Glass* by Alice Huelett Metz

MG *Yesterdays Milkglass Today* by Regis and Mary Ferson

MK *Complete Book of McKee Glass* by Sandra McPhee Stout

MKVG *M'Kee Victorian Glass (Catalogues 1859-1871)*

MMPG *Pattern Glass* by Mollie McCain

NOVA *Nova Scotia Glass* by George Mac Claren

NM *New Martinsville Glass Story* by Everett R. and Addie R. Miller

OPA *Opaque Glass* by S. T. Millard

P&L *The Lion & the Peacock* by Sheilegh Murray

PAT *Patents & Patterns* by Arthur Peterson

PC *Paden City the Color Company* by Jerry Barnett

PG&B *American Pressed Glass & Figural Bottles* by A. C. Revi

PITT *Pittsburgh Glass 1797-1891* by Lowell Innes

PP1 *Patterns & Pinafores - Pressed Glass Toy Dishes Vol. 1 and 2*
PP2 by Marion Hartung and Ione Huesham

RIV *Riverside Glass Works of Wellsburg, W. Va. 1879-1907* by C. W. Gorham

RS *Ruby Stained Pattern Glass* by Richard Carber Barret

SAN1 *The Glass Industry in Sandwich - Vol. 1* by Raymond E. Barlow and Joan E. Kaiser

SAN3 *The Glass Industry in Sandwich - Vol. 3* by Raymond E. Barlow and Joan E. Kaiser

SW1 *Spinning Wheel - Dec., 1958 Letters p. 8*

SW2 *Spinning Wheel - May, 1975 "English Pressed Glass Manufacturer - Henry Greener & Co., Wear Flint Glass Works"* by A. C. Revi

SW3 *Spinning Wheel - March, 1977 "Triangular Prism"* by Robert S. Troutman Sr.

TAR *Tarentum Pattern Glass* by Robert Lucas

TOY *Toy Glass* by Doris Anderson Lechler

WEPG *Pressed Glass in America* by John and Elizabeth Welker

WHPG *Wallace-Homestead Price Guide to Pattern Glass* edited by Dori Miles and Robert W. Miller

INDEX

A

B

I

J

K

L

M

R

S